A Field Negroes Handbook

A Field Negroes Handbook

Napoleon Wells

iUniverse, Inc.
New York Lincoln Shanghai

A Field Negroes Handbook

iUniverse books may be ordered through booksellers or by contacting:

iUniverse
2021 Pine Lake Road, Suite 100
Lincoln, NE 68512
www.iuniverse.com
1-800-Authors (1-800-288-4677)

ISBN: 0-595-33947-6

Printed in the United States of America

Contents

...TO MY BROTHERS ON THEIR PERFECTIONS............1

PARCHMENT 5

CURRENCY 7

SEPTEMBER..11

...TO MY PEERS ON PRETENTIOUSNESS pt 1 12

SHOW THEM LOVE......................................17

HEAL...19

SAID I 24

THIS IS AN OBLIGATION? 26

REPORTING LIVE.......................................30

THIS HAS A TITLE 33

...THE REVOLUTION MUST BE.............................35

I WILL NAME THIS LATER 39

...TO ALL THE MASTERS OF ILLUSION 41

THE CORNER COMETH...................................45

DIG IT..48

DOYOUKNOWWHATIMSAYINDOYOUKNOWWHATIMEAN. 50

TO MY PEERS ON PRETENTIOUSNESS pt 2 52

VIGILANCE IN AFTERTHOUGHT.........................55

NORTHBOUND-SOUTHBOUND 56

THE INDICTMENT. 59

NEWS AT 11 62

VAPOR. 64

THE WRITING IS ON YOUR FALL. 66

HOPELESS. 68

3rd FLOOR APARTMENT 70

...TO OUR MOTHERS 72

HATRED WRITTEN IN MESPEAK 1. 74

ASK YOURSELF: THE ATHEIST 76

I wish to thank George, Sharon and Deidra for listening to my rantings, my people for giving me so much guidance and sight by just living, the most high for leading me to share this part of myself and all of the truly wonderful people from all walks of life that I have met on my journey (NYC, ATL, Bingo....). Think and be free.

...TO MY BROTHERS ON THEIR PERFECTIONS

I wondered aloud just the other day about what your reaction to being told you are "beautifully perfect" would be. What initially occurred to me was that such a compliment would be seen as rather unusual but has stuck with me as I have watched you make efforts to gain footing in your life as long as I have been in it. My watching of you fraternize has enforced this idea repeatedly and brought me to the point that I am now at, where I feel that your perfections do at times get the better of you. Is it that you are intimidated by them? Are you worried that the expectations of your perfection are too high? How can that be when after having the ground pulled from beneath in one way or another for so many generations you still manage to find a place to stand. Unsteady at times, yes, but you do indeed stand. I should admit that I am wonderfully impressed with your perfections and how you wear them like a second skin (could it be to disguise the first skin?).

Getting back to where I began, you are indeed a collection of small perfections. I watched as you played with your children in St. James Park on Thursday. They had absolute looks of elation on their faces. Where else in the world would they have wanted to be but right where daddy was swinging them? You being there to elevate your children on the swings was interesting to me. Each time they came down, and they of course had to eventually come back down, you were there to raise them. And to this observer at least, it appeared to be your pleasure to do it. What stuck with me about the picture that you and your children painted for me on that crisp day was the background. Not even thirty yards from where you had created this bubble of joy to house your children in were other members of the fraternity who apparently lost their way. The bright smiles and warm clothing that you had wrapped your children in were not to be seen on these brothers, but I don't wish to focus on them for right now. Even were they not to admit it, they saw you just like I did, and like them I envied the kind of closeness that I saw you share with those two little ones. We have not and do not embrace each other often enough. Maybe our fear is that too much contact

1

between skin that is so feared and wondered at may bring attention (and we know what happens when we bring attention to ourselves).

Seeing you elevating your children skyward is a perfection in that there are those who believe that you do not have the strength in your arms or character to do so. Popular rhetoric indicates that your self destructiveness and selfishness can and do eventually get the better of you, and long before you are able to be of any benefit to your children in their lives, or on their swings, or at their schools or in their happiness. I wanted to walk over and talk to you right then and there and ask about this small perfection. This perfection that you were sharing with your little ones and radiating outward toward those brothers nearby. With your shine, how could we not see you. And how could I not see you. How can they all not see you.

I have wondered how it is that you function so easily with such weight on your shoulders. How do you still manage to harness the perfection of not only holding your head high, but strutting to and fro. Fences have been erected around your home and yet I still see a glint in your eye that tells me "not long now". Freedom to you is just being able to look at your children laugh at the support of your hand at their back while they fly and they return again, only to be launched again. They seek your guidance, to learn from and avoid your mistakes and they are launched again. Your children hear the whispers of failure that are tied to their legacy and then they see you strive and demand excellence and push yourself and struggle and they are launched again.

Like many around you, I understand that what is at the heart of your perfection is a kind of rebellion against imperfection. Being flawed and average is not your way. Your willingness to acknowledge that you need the help and often times guidance of your woman is amazing to me. That she can see through all of the muck and into your truly perfect inner is amazing and a testament to her beauty. I have watched you in school and to see you run away from your destiny often worries me, but the greatest of all of us had to first realize that a certain level of arrogance is necessary to achieve that greatness. You have every right to be afraid in that those among you that seek the greatest gains must often sacrifice parts of their greater selves for lesser safeties. When you refuse to speak the king's English in his court what you are saying is that what is most important to you is relating to those in your fraternity and tribe. I admire your desire in this matter, and I wonder if you really understand how your perfection in speaking is communicating and voicing your concerns affects us all. Some are threatened by the strength of your voice and its resolve. At times, it seems that you raise your voice so much that you are simply screaming for the hell of it, but again, even I may misunderstand you at those times.

I watch how you interact with educators and I see what has been done to you and I am glad that another perfection within you lets you battle on. There are signs everywhere in your young surroundings and in your homes that there is no way for you to succeed in the endeavor of education, and yet there are those with enough of the perfection you have in your veins to fight through this. I am certain that there are times when even your other tribe members say and do things that may fill you with self doubt. You and I have both experienced it. Many among us have grown to associate the use of the mind in pursuit of knowledge with being something that we are not. When has perfection ever not included the development of the intellect. I thank and salute you for being perfect enough to avoid falling into that trap.

To be born who and what you are in this land and to have the audacity to think of yourself as a protector and provider for your family, concerned citizen and contributor to your society, creator of arts, molder of minds….all of these you have been even with chains of one kind or another upon you. I imagine that you could say that this is a fan letter, and in a sense it is, for I am privileged to be among this fraternity with all of it's' imperfections. We do not look upon the lake and see our perfection in our reflection as beauty. In too many instances it is we brothers, who are threatened by it. The perfection that is that man's rich hued skin has on too many occasions been broken by force applied by other black skin. It may be that these overwhelming perfections of the mind and body and spirit are what cause us to be so destructive. Everyone wants to hold onto something beautiful and sacred…we as a species are a collector of rare and beautiful things, so instead of allowing our beautiful perfection to roam untamed we ourselves seek to reign in it by destroying it through self hatred by word and by deed, others want to cage it and be amused and entertained by our perfections. The perfect silk of our voices mesmerizes those who listen, they obsess over ways to harness and later own it. The perfect gifts given to us physically are marveled at, we are celebrated in the use of our bodies over our minds, the sight of our perfect nakedness provokes confusion, violence and all manner of emotional chaos.

This is not something that you and I should be threatened by. It is a part of our birthright. The perfection we possess scares and preserves us, it moves us to action for and against ourselves, our communities and our lands. Know that I stand in awe of how truly perfect your walk and talk are. I am moved by how perfect your love for your children is. We haven't embraced in a time, and as I have indicated it may be that you and I too are afraid of touching some of your perfection and allowing you to be in intimate contact with some of my own. But without that closeness, there is no way to ever get to the point where we can breed love into the equation of living with our perfections. Without that embrace we will always be prisoners of one kind or another. Brothers I will be home shortly, my love goes out to you. Do not fear being perfect, let your tears spill for what has been given to you in your life, allow tenderness to enter your most perfect of hearts and hold your family to you, incredibly tightly, they need to bask in the light that is your perfection. We are all glad to have you.

PARCHMENT

So as I write this piece on this piece of parchment and page
I seek peace and pray for wisdom in spite of my age
I humbly ask for direction from my sage and for hard work in life for no wage
...though they in those streets turn a blind eye to my stride I see that the battle is waged
...fill this page with ammo in the element of my rage, my rage against this machine
of ignorance forces me to disengage...from BET....from GOP....from my half naked
sister and Air Force One asshole on channel 23
from the less than ignorant, more than a nigga, Black man from NYC
from the commercialism that requires you break bank to place product under your tree
from the wrong prayers said while on bended knee
from the sister who only offered her bodies sustenance and life and the brother
who lives in his city's housing "project" and drives turbo Z3
See, three days ago I was given this page and a commission to speak
...to speak about the people face, not seeing that in their hands they hold this earth like a ball
they won't listen to reason until after you have run with and for that ball...there...
and shot that ball...
without seeing that brother run from that court and get shot for the gall
his blood is upon the playing surface and they seek to clean it before young eyes see
their reflection in it
Blood is a permanent stain as is the memory of it
...that child will have a mental sketch of what they see
see me struggle daily to make it
see you smile and tell corner cat it's all good while when I see him I smile and fake it

see that cat touch his sister where she is sacred
see the appeal of that corner and offer innocence and no chance to make it (out alive)
make it a double or a triple
cuz five years down the road youth inherits corner with cousin the Crip and homeboy who is crippled
now his so called girlchildfriend is pregnant
so now poverty ripples
the effects do anyway
she is expecting any day
landed corner gentry youth has no money put away
picked up guns and his toys are put away
caught by storm troopers and four years put away
will come back man-child with even less direction
still packs heat like radiator in his slum for protection
girlchildfriend starts to expose herself physically, has no idea of how to expose herself emotionally, closed up too tight....saves thoughts but gives away sacred
all her happiness gone too, world of mine please take it....
...head of homeland security won't secure my home
too occupied with the practice of calling it broken
doesn't see that he forced me and mine to this guest house in his yard
when I come to the table he introduces me to Ralph and MBU.S.A. and tells me while
they are stripping me that they mean me no harm
while he cleanses the minds of my children
pulls out his billfold and convinces my women that it is bigger and better than mine
and keeps me preoccupied with running and shooting.....and smiling for the camera
we all see it.....we all read it.....we all know it.....we all live it.....we all try to forget it....we all hurt from it.....we have all watched it....we have all walked over it.....we have

CURRENCY

Anything that we acknowledge as being a disadvantage to us in our lives can and will be used as currency by us or by someone who shares this perceived disadvantage. I say perceived disadvantage because largely the obstacles that we face over the course of our lives and their severity is in the eye of the beholder. Imagine the surprise for an Asian girl, with a physical disability, born to two uneducated parents in the Midwest. Were she to follow the lead of those who attribute success or failure to the isms (racism, sexism, heterosexism…) then she should quit while she is ahead and wait to be filed away in the "hopeless failure" category.

This of course, would be an error on her part and is a continued error on the part of many of those who are trying to change the antiquated thinking of the society in which we live. Understand, I am not saying that those who are racially and ethnically different than the majority are not scrutinized and often aggressed against because of racial differences, I am however saying that this difference is often used as a reason behind every failure that an individual experiences.

This currency is spent by both the majority and emerging majority communities in American society. Your child didn't get into an Ivy League institution? It must be because there are an abundance of Mau Mau and Aztec students taking over the campuses of the nation's institutions of higher learning. At no point has there been any evidence provided to support these concerns, but the idea remains that the dreaded specter of affirmative action hangs over head. As a nation, our mouths work aggressively on both sides of our heads when lip service is paid to the idea of giving the underprivileged a chance to share in the workings of the American progress machine, but we cannot come to a consensus about where, when and how these opportunities should be provided.

Do we really need to have controls in place to ensure that fairness in hiring practices and college and university admission policies is enforced? Of course we do. How have you gotten a number of the jobs that you have worked in your lifetime? Before you begin to list your myriad qualifications to work any and every private sector position imaginable, I want you to consider that in many instances you likely had a friend bring a position to your attention or you were told by a neighbor or friend of your family. The greater the influence and access that your family has to university and employment administrators then the greater your chances of getting the positions in both work and college enrollment that you desire. Now consider that your family socioeconomically disadvantaged, without the access to university officials. Without access to human resources representatives. Without influence. In many instances you would be shut out of any opportunity even if you were qualified. Do you still wish to argue the fairness of circumstances?

Why would I wish Argentina to cry for an individual who has been privileged to have several different kinds of access and influence which have provided them with greater privilege? Suppose I live with a number of writers. At any time in my social network I can ask about the process of writing, I can ask for advice on bettering my own skills as a scribe and even take an apprenticeship within that network. This set of circumstances has afforded me every opportunity to be a writer. My body of work should be looked at closely because of the advantages afforded me in my surroundings. If my body of work were then compared to someone who has had no formal training as a writer and no access to trained and published writers then what should be judged on their part is potential. If their body of work has quality which is close to that of an individual who has the aforementioned advantages then a discerning eye should see how the second writer would do if they had those same advantages. If they had the formal training and the writers to ask questions of and work with, they too might have displayed the same kind of quality as a writer.

Taken another way, if you are running a 100 meter dash and are provided with a 20 meter head start in the race you are fully expected to win. And not just slightly, but comfortably. If there is another racer who makes the race competitive, and comes within a few meters of defeating you in that race, then I as an observer would like to see the race run again without the 10 meter advantage. I would want to see every runner beginning at the same starting line, out of the blocks all at once and then we will all have a better sense of which the best of all the sprinters truly is. I think of affirmative action as a way of identifying who the best sprinters are among those who did not begin the race with a ten meter lead. I regret that those who are born with the lead feel penalized, but as competitors, their spirit should drive them to test themselves. But those are the thoughts of a dreamer.

Fairness, equal standing and competition are not what the privileged actually want. A life of privilege may lead to feelings of entitlement, and then ten meter lead will then be assumed to be a birthright. Who wants to give ground with the race on the line? As I said, lip service is what we so readily pay out, we do not, as a nation, believe in the benefits of identifying potentially successfully students and employees in the gray area of not having had the access and privilege. We cling to the idea that black and white must and should rule our decisions.

Which brings me back to the currency of race and other hot button topics in our land. Though it is an issue, one that we must face (there is no such thing as a completely unprejudiced person) how much of an effect does it have on the standing of your life every day? Are you limiting yourself, refusing to do battle because your fear (excuse) is that the ceiling of race will prohibit your success? Consider the very real influence of socioeconomic status in our society. An African-American from a family with a combined income of six figures is likely going to have an academic resume which most closely resembles the academic resume of a White American student whose family has a combined income ranging in six figures. The finances are what afford the access. The African American within that family has parents with careers that they are able to access, a social network that can provide greater influence and the means to pursue an education above those offered by public schools. An African American living below the poverty line in Baltimore is likely going to have an academic resume which resembles that of a White student from the Appalachians. Their experience is linked through poverty and that poverty is what keeps them from having the access and influence.

To discuss this idea further, the poorest areas in most cities (urban centers) are still inhabited by Black and Brown citizens and socioeconomic status in that regard is largely tied into race and ethnicity. Your chances of being poor or disadvantaged are greater if you are African American. With all of the social obstacles that come with living in urban centers (high crime rates, drug abuse, failing school systems), I would look at a student who managed to grow and prosper as being one who could potentially succeed in an environment that promotes educational advancement. If you were to remove the distractions of violence, poor in home living conditions, poor health and nutrition and poor schooling how might these students perform? Considering that they performed well when given all of those distractions, they might flourish if those factors are taken out of their lives and off of their consciences. That is at the heart of offering opportunities.

Race is a matter of importance in our society still and that we both spend it as currency to convince others that we have been treated unfairly, what we are not doing is considering what about race and race matters are tied into other parts of experience, like a probable lack of exposure and poverty. We must work outside of ourselves to ensure that we are fostering hope and potential so that there will be less of an emphasis placed on race for our societies failures. If we continue to cry wolf when it comes to race or use it entirely too loosely, then when we really are confronted with a matter of race and discrimination we will find that our sense of it is culturally bankrupt.

SEPTEMBER

She walked into my life sometime in September and without even realizing, she
set up shop and forced open my welded mind with her bad self and so....
...at least three times a day whether I find the sun kissing
my cheekbone or rain draping my eyelids
I set out mouthing to a mystery God on
how I feel about her....but about means in the vicinity of and I
assure you that some of me has always existed somewhere inside of her from that
fateful day in September when she walked into my living space
and shook my hand and I immediately understood that it
was indeed her
she who was conceived sometime before time and God simply created my world
and let it evolve in preparation for her arrival
And I was one of those lucky enough to be born into her world and given baked
skin and eyes like her own
and hair so tough that my unborn children hang onto it
and laugh and eat a meal she prepares with care
and fall into slumber from stories she tells about our ancestors (the ancestors like
those tales too)
who sung songs while bent over in the heat of their day, and fought and won and
lost and lived and are living....
....and their living stands as a means of praying and all I'm saying is...
Letting her know what I know might scare her
but she should know it
I should show it
I have cultivated this life of she and I and we should grow it
It is her world and I am grateful that she knows that I am in it

... TO MY PEERS ON PRETENTIOUSNESS pt 1

Sitting while listening to my Ursula Rucker CD, brooding more so than listening and wondering what Che' would do at a time like this. Though there is very little that is unique about this moment, brooding makes me feel as if there must be some sort of action taken. I after all am a student and there is no time like my matriculated years to get all of my political agendas on the table. It is entirely possible that the answer will come to me if I look into Che's face on my t-shirt. I decide that the action that I must take is to approach many of my fellow "revolutionaries" on campus and talk about taking action against those who are in positions of power and involve themselves directly in the oppression of the rest of us. Namely the poor, uneducated, racially and sexually different and women.

Even worse than the numbing presence of the oppressor is the brain-washing that has taken place within our generation, making us almost oblivious to these injustices. We are so involved on campus that we go out of our way to make our needs and voices heard. We have staged protests by the student union in addition to recruiting lecturers who bring the truth about the injustices to the fascist administration that would rather we just go away.

Our crown jewel had to be hip-hop culture week and it was here where we were able to unite all of the fragmented, politically driven groups on campus. Though we didn't have the opportunity to dialogue, my set felt that it was encouraging that we could all come together in the same place and not have any major arguments or old beefs emerge.

All of these myriad matters are running through my mind as I begin to load my day's needs into the guitar bag that doubles as my knapsack (military fatigue guitar bag I might add). My abnormal psych book took of the majority of the space and I slipped in a note to be sure to remember to call my dad about the deposit that he promised to put into my account, he has been late the past few times.

My vintage ball cap doesn't look tattered enough so I take some time with a pair of scissors and meat tenderizer to get it just right. This is a new cap and so it will take some time to get it to where it should be. Before facing the cold shoulder of the world for the day I give myself one final look and decide that a few things have to be changed immediately. I elect to change my Che top in favor of one with Huey Newton on it. I change my blue Chuck Taylor's for a pair of blue Kangaroos and I rub on some Egyptian musk. All warriors must have their armor on when they are preparing to face the enemy.

My guitar bag feels lighter than usual and it catches my eye just as I am locking my dorm door that the MC5 sticker on my bag is looking a little tattered. Additionally, my "Bush is a sinner" sticker is getting a little worn for wear. No matter, they stand for something and I will keep them as long as I possibly can.

The union is a five minute walk from my dorm community and I know that many of my revolutionary associates will be in our appointed place. We had agreed to meet up at some point during the day to discuss the latest revolutionary work that we were reading, "Blood in my eye" by George Jackson. My arrival was trumpeted by a lively debate on where we can go after having protested the continuous conflict in the Middle East. It was a freezing cold day when we had the demonstration, but many of us realized the victory and support for the cause that were brought about as a result of the demonstration.

We were a group of over twenty that referred to ourselves as the Forward Thinkers. At any one time, there would be five or six different, splintered conversations/debates/exchanges taking place if we were assembled. Taking a once around before being seated, I found that some among us were disturbed at the way in which our groups involvement and purpose was being questioned in one of the campus papers and several of the organizations echoed this sentiment. Jeremy, one of our senior members was in the middle of a thought.

"Nah, we are the voice of the people on campus. They don't have a voice here without us. The people are hip-hop culture. How are they going to play our hip-hop week like that?"

I glanced at the paper and saw that Jeremy was referring to some unflattering statements that were made about our freestyle competition winner, our DJ battle and our graffiti artist appreciation day. The writer believed that the blond haired, blue eyes winner of the freestyle battle was favored by the crowd less so for his skills lyrically and more so for his pigment actually.

It would be a lie if I said that I didn't feel some of it at the battle. The guy came up and introduced himself as "Danger" and then indicated that he was "born in Vermont" although much of his youth was spent in the presence of poor blacks in "Hartford, Connecticut". It was in Hartford that the spirit of lyrical know-how possessed his body and carried him into battle after battle where he emerged victorious. In the four rounds of the tournament he faced one Black MC and three white ones who all had similar stories relating to their growth as MCs. The writer mused, "Black people have obviously become very accepting of privileged white people moving into our communities to take up apprenticeships as rappers".

Mind you, I am not saying that the fix was in, but I fear that the crowd was largely swayed by many of the White MCs on stage. In the all White MC battle final, the crowd seemed to be almost torn. Another point highlighted by the scathing article before me. I guess I feel that in the spirit of the battle was in putting out hip-hop culture as a form of revolution and White people should be active in all parts of social revolution as well, shouldn't they.

The writer continued on and outlined what they felt was the remarkable failure of our staged protest. His appreciation of it went as follows; "None of the scheduled "community leaders" attended the protest and the signs and slogans developed for the occasion by the organizers largely went unnoticed. Why are these wealthy students trying to present themselves as having a kinship with the poor who roam the outside of this campuses' gates? The very idea of this ragtag group of misinformed zealots is amusing". Needless to say the remainder of the article was less flattering that the parts that I had just read.

Jeremy, being a young white man, always made it his business to show outrage at the way in which the white members of our group were treated by many in the campus community. He stopped short of calling it reverse racism, but my sense was that he was tempted to do just that. Many within that community questioned why Jeremy wore dreadlocks, kept Mandela and X posters all over his room listened to only Dead Prez in his Mercedes. I had met Jeremy's parents both of who were physicians and the discomfort they felt among us socially was clear. Jeremy was from Tarzana, California and no one could directly identify where his battle against injustice began.

He was an excellent Computer Science student and would often talk about wanting to infiltrate the "ivory tower" at the top of his discipline and change the culture of Comp Sci. He and I never got as far as deciding how he might go about doing that but I am sure that his plan was sound.

The attacks on our group seemed to be from ignorance from where I stood. That was always the story with revolution though. People were very rarely ready for change, so the agents of change were often the targets of undue criticism. We were no different, maybe those around us figured that the many cultures represented within our group made us weak, I felt that it strengthened us. Many voices adding to the volume of our protest is how I often looked at it.

Tania, a Hawaiian who also wore dreadlocks, was my romantic interest in our group and many of the Black students on campus would snicker at us and some had taken it upon themselves to make lewd comments in drunken moments (at least I think that they were drunken moments). She had arrived and after a brief embrace (what we call our Karma Touch) she too was wrapped up in the debates around us. She had often indicated that we in fact had no real purpose outside of listening to music, smoking herb and making plans that we never quite got around to. Tania went so far as to accuse many of our comrades as being involved only for the sake of saying that they were around "others", and please do not make me explain what she means by others (you appear to be a wise enough sort that such an explanation would insult your intelligence).

Again, I would not be completely honest if I did not say here that such thoughts had played across my gray matter a time or two. There were instances in which it seemed to me that the kinds of exchanges that I found myself standing in the midst of, even the kind of relationship that I was a partner in, were entered into under false pretenses.

Even while I cared a great deal for Tania and I wanted to foster a growth between us, she and I would often talk about the absence of striving Black men in the lives of Black women and children. We would go on for hours about how positive male influence was needed in "the community" and how she thought that I was ideal for children for just that reason. But....here I am dating a woman who is a physical, social or economic member of that community. How much of an influence could I really be.....the more I think about it, I have never even dated any of the "sisters" on campus. Not that they don't appeal to me....it just hasn't happened.

My feeling has always been that the sisters felt that my style was cornball. And they have reacted to me in that way. I am from Hawthorne, NY and I don't have a "New York" accent of any kind, and even the way in which I speak is made fun of. Always has been. I don't get it really. Is it what I say or how I sound when I say it that matters most? I guess it is a combination of both. Even a revolutionary has to be entertaining. I never started growing 'locks because my sense of their purpose is that in the lives of Rastafarians is religious. It would be insulting for me to wear them if I were not spiritually connected to them. But there are those among us who wear them for fashion. To each his own.

The men who I see with them are often on campus with White women, but I get grilled because I am walking around with an Asian woman who talks and looks a little different? How ridiculous is that. Her spirit is actually in making change in the world and yet her skin is what people focus on first and only, our relationship is treated as if it were a transgression. I don't get it really. All many of us want to do is help, but we are generally laughed at or antagonized.

Several of our friends had been jumped at parties and our response has always been one of peace. Jeremy went so far as to explain that we can't blame the Black students on campus for hating us, after they had spent "their entire lives under the heel of the oppressor". I'm not sure I agree. I am spending my every free moment trying to free the mind of my community from being under that heel and my reward is a beat down? You must be fucking kidding me…

My clothes and musical taste were often the target of jest and I could get over that in the long run, by why was it such a big deal to begin with? I listened to whoever sounded right to me at any given time, but it seemed like the only way to have any real acceptance was to have a collection of Black artists only. What of the Black artists who contributed to the problems of our communities thinking by advocating murder, apathy and consumerism. I get offended that it is normal for any Black person anywhere to listen to that garbage.

I don't remember what we spoke about for the remainder of the day because my head was largely elsewhere. I was planning a poem to write about some of my thoughts and I was going to write a tune that would be played with our band at the next Slam session. Inside of me were many things that we making a volcanic trip to the surface. The time had come to tackle the problem head on even if it meant getting into it with my own people. I wasn't afraid. I understood that the spirit of true revolutionaries was behind me.

I bid a farewell of sorts to my comrades as I prepared to make my way to Abnormal Psych, but first I wanted to run home and change back into my Che' shirt. I was also a touch hungry so I will pick up a soy burger and some brown rice while I am there. Revolution is hungry business after all.

SHOW THEM LOVE

So you show them love
Choose in sound mind and round behind to grow them love
Do they even acknowledge
that you show them love
that you sold yourself short to be his mistress to show them love
love supreme
love like you compete to make his team
love like you ignore me though I scream
like this is a bad dream
well a nightmare
and look at me puzzled like why do I care
You show them love in a two seater with 20 inches
A TV in the headrest and a navigation system which led them
to that alley where you swallowed his babies and they later drop
you off...and dip without so much as an I love you...
....from them
You show them love after seeing his brand (where is it on his flesh?)
And he touched your hand and demanded attention
not to mention five minutes of your time
and you didn't consider the lifetime of hardship
or my changing opinion of you....over them
They who have four children with 3 separate women and are juggling
two women at one time
they
you show love
and I witness it
You show them love after a game winning shot
at an after hours spot
giggling at how blinding their very person is
and reason that the flock of sisterbirds
and flow of love must be necessity

make them worthy of love
You feed them love sweet cakes
even though they treat you as
nothing more than a commodity
a perk maybe
You stand there and show them love
fall broken down and tow love
become bitter and wonder if they even know love
seeing that hate is one level below love
but I can't stop you so you go love
You show them love, them?!?
What manner of love is that?
You show them love
They who have forgotten your name and call you everything but
they who weaken your tribe and wouldn't recognize you if you struck them down
(wishful thinking on my part)
No longer do I intend to fight you about it
remember it was me in my biased \unloved confusion who called you on it
that's what love is though

HEAL

Mama had a gun and did the only thing that the misguided and lost do with such a powerful tool and limited options. She went out and got it two weeks ago and though she was lost, she managed to find her way to the very place where she located her brand new automatically, and automatically assumed that the possession of this tool would offer her a kind of freedom, cause she sure couldn't get much from yen hour work days, children who forgot how to thank her for the meals that she threw together on aching arches in front of a barely working stove and a husband who had revolutionized the concept of "taking someone for granted".

Mama had a gun and never really knew whether she was supposed to turn it on the world (her enemy) or herself (her enemy).

Papa used to love her. So he took the time to bring out her lighthouse of a smile and talk about how deep the wellspring of his feelings were for her and he just as quickly turned his back and covered that well and seemed to want to drown out the light in that smile when the little ones arrived. When the daughter and sons arrived. When he had a job that supported the whole family and they all thrived. Until he began to talk about how trapped he was by this woman he once claimed to love with all of these "little college educated niggas" coming in and taking his and other jobs and he became expendable (was he ever not expendable?) and soon it was so sorry but we can't keep you Mr. Mitchell and papa began to wonder out loud about her getting "knocked up" purposely and keeping him from going to college even though papa never liked school and how was he ever going to get through anyway and wasn't he the one who said that he didn't "need college no way" and went on and took that job and started loving his wife and making the very babies that they both needed to care for and what did she have to do with the college boys? And papa seemed so happy when the daughter and sons arrived and talked at length about caring so intensely for his little ones....their little ones and he began to turn to the bottom of that bottle of brown potion for answers to the questions that he kept asking and mama couldn't answer and he started taking out those frustrations on men who were half the man that he was and sometimes got stopped in his tracks by men who were twice as angry and had even less answers than he did and how could mama have the answers when she was being swept under just like he was and how could papa not see that if he drowned than she and their little ones who he loved so dearly went down with him and how could papa lose all of that love that he had for her and how could he stop being warmed by that light of hers…that light that he would hurry home for that light that he would destroy worlds and doubts for that light that he once told his best friends that he would kill for…

What did mama have to do to get that love back she had changed her hair and clothes and bought that scent that he loved so much and that meal (because the way to a man's heart is through his stomach) and it seemed that the more she smiled the more he said that she was mocking his failure well that is least what she was able to get from him in that he always expressed himself with rage and anger and tension and she wondered what kind of happiness and comfort he found at the bottom of that bottle of potion and she could swear that there were nights when he would be talking to that bottle and where was papa getting the money for his magical elixir since he had lost his job and why wouldn't he come up out of his haze long enough to help her with the children who he claimed to love so very much even in those times when he would mutter about "sticking around for the kids" and mama couldn't help but notice how much junior started to look like papa and like papa he wouldn't listen to her much anymore and since he got a few whiskers on his face he too didn't seem to want to talk to her and like papa she wondered where he was getting all of his answers from because he certainly wasn't asking her and did he have a beautiful brown potion/woman/lover who gave him what he needed?

She had very rarely ever heard anyone she knew use the word hate in her presence but in the last month junior and papa had both aimed the word at her and had been certain to hit the mark and even though she knew this man and this child who she had loved both and raised both and cared for both and lived with both and laughed with both she did not recognize either of them now or the pain that made the two of them curl into a fist from fear but lash out and attack the one person who could understand what they were facing and actually wanted to face it with them both how could her husband want to go at it alone when they agreed to share all things why could he not tell her about this affair that he was carrying on with the bottle and why had he quit and given up why was he so frozen in the face of this threat to the well being of his family mama was willing to fight at all costs and her partner had decided to lay down his life and sacrifice it to a god somewhere at the bottom of a bottle a god who had so obviously forsaken him that one would think that papa would give his prayers up and set the bottle down and look at the life that he is stealing from junior and his daughter and younger son and mama who still stood firmly within her bubble of loving papa and believed fully that it was only a matter of time before he got over his addiction to the potion and went out and secured a living for his family and took back his pride and loved his children and checked their homework and greased his boys heads before church service and fixed their bikes and wrap their gifts before putting them under the tree but papa said that there would be no more of that holiday in their home and mama had to get the gifts herself finding the time to get them between working two shifts and trying to keep the roof firmly attached over their heads and the lights on and the light in her smile and comfort herself because the soul of the one she had given her life to was poisoned by the potion he clung to…

How was mama making her self feel as lovely and cherished as she used to when papa loved her and how could he stop loving her? Did love work that way? And why hadn't papa told that if he knew it all along?

The doubt in her daughters eyes stabbed at mama every time she had to see her daughter, their daughter asking papa about a gift or a new pretty dress that mama had bought and papa's only response was to ask about how much the dress cost and what in the hell did she need another dress for when she had so many already and her daughter, their daughter would ask papa if she was pretty, beautiful, the prettiest, most beautiful girl in the world and papa was often off in his own world somewhere off on a journey that the keeper of that bottle sent him off to and mama doubted if he even heard their daughter's question and she began to try and comfort her daughter who had a look of shame that matched her own for not being able to draw papa out of his maze and into their home and out of his own hate and into their love and how could she blame herself when she was one of the best things to ever happen to papa even if he didn't know it at that very moment and would he ever know it again how could mama tell him if he never stopped talking to he or she or they in the bottle long enough to hear her voice and would he know what to do when he heard it would it make him any difference was papa the man she remembered after having been a refugee in the bottle so long

Papa used to sing to his youngest son, their youngest son at night when his breathing was it's shallowest and neither papa or mama had any answer and papa began to ask of the bottle why he didn't have the money and why mama didn't have the money and how could his child, their child be given the burden of coming into this world without the ability to breath long and well enough to enjoy the beauty of the scents around him or to run around and live comfortably within his childhood and how could his life be taken from him at an exponential rate when he had just been blessed with it not even four years before and maybe papa believed that if he offered himself to whatever god it was he prayed to in those quiet moments of his then this deity would show mercy and spare their child but how did the prayers fall on deaf ears from above (below in the bottle) and papa would cry on many an evening alone and ask why he couldn't be granted the strength to save his little one from this fate his little one who had not even had the chance to demonstrate any of his potential in this world even if the world wouldn't have any part of him papa loved him and all those private moments were spent in worse pain for papa than a congested chest or staggered breathing and mama tried to help papa see that baby's condition was not his fault but he kept pointing to the fact those "folks cross town never have they hospitals filled with they dying children, and you know it!" but to mama this didn't make a difference because the hurt in papa's eyes was enough to make her believe that the man's pain would be fuel and air and support for their son and get him through and he could still pull through but papa's pain had turned to self pity and their son, their youngest child, the product of their love was fading...

And papa kept stringing together a sequence of tales wherein she was responsible for the world which she saw crumbling on all sides and she asked her family and there were no answers that any of them could offer and they never liked papa anyway and her children weren't as bright as everyone else's and why had she moved into that neighborhood with papa and why did she stay with papa when all he did was lay around all day he at least used to act like a man but he wasn't anybody's real man now and she did this to herself and why could they not see what she and he and they were going through and that they really were trying to make it and papa was just overwhelmed by all of it and ya'll should know how it is out here for our men and mama's mother told her that she should have married that other boy because he was so nice and maybe none of them saw what was happening with mama the desperate look in her eyes and how much she wanted to get pass this because her preacher told her that all trials will pass and this was one that will too pass and when would mama get over it and she started to cry and even thought about going out and getting her own bottle of potion and sitting next to papa and taking up a vigil and praying and even considered that offer from her co-worker who said that she is so beautiful and she hadn't heard that from the voice of papa that she was so familiar with and she decided to try and ignore it but junior got arrested just the other day and a judge, the judge called the home that she was trying to hold together broken and her daughter seemed to be talking to herself more than papa and had done away with her toys and they youngest continued to fade and fade and fade...

And she spoke to the smiling face in the pawn shop and explained to him that he knew how it was in the neighborhood and how she could really use something to protect herself because you know how it is and he sold her a powerful tool, a decision maker that had been brought it just a few days prior and she tucked in her little girl, their little girl and went to see her son, their son and watched as he was led off and her son, their son, she prayed over and told papa to do the same and she locked the bathroom door and made a decision...her decision.

SAID I

Why you hate me...
said the nigger to Officer Krupkey while he lay face down
on the side of the road looking in the face of his son
realizing that this peacekeeper done just told his
little one he aint shit,
and anytime he comes in late his woman can't help
but spouting all the next day about how hw aint
shit in front of his son and he watches his little man's tears
stream down his face and he holds his hands tight like daddy taught him
but even the Most high won't take this cops' foot off of daddy's neck so even
the Almighty is telling him daddy aint shit and little man gon have to grow up
and be a daddy someday and drive this same road with somebody on patrol
and his son with em
and God watching

Why you don't love me
said the negress to the buck as he stalked
by in a throwback jersey
but he thinks so much like a throwback
that he should be rockin a rucksack with 1848 on the back
and a chain round his neck....
and his wrists....
and his feet....
And he posts up on the block....auction
to get his teeth checked to see if he can smile real big
for the cameras but he didn't hear her question
and never will
cuz if she aint undressed, he aint hollerin
but she has always fully exposed herself
trying to protect him from a harsh world and all he does
to thank her is tell her where her flaws are

frown at where her scars are…though he dun gave her some of em
so now she fends for herself and she doesn't ask no questions
cuz he can't hear em no way

Why you can't see me
said the bruised ego to the perpetrator as he went on to school
and watched her sachet off in this man's whip,
his hand on her hip
and bruised ego on the side already saw the outcome of this one
her tears tomorrow
and the next month
still overlooking him for unworthy suitors not built to nurture
so he stacks grade A
gets enough experience and gets great pay
and so here she finally sees him near and clear and he can't stand to look upon
her damaged face
too hurt himself from being ignored

Why you think you don't need me
said the brown to the blue eye
looking in the mirror at one side of the face spiting the other
thinking out loud that none can see me but to hate me
and I refuse to say that this is life

THIS IS AN OBLIGATION?

Being a committed sports fan is much like entering into a marriage. Once you have signed a pact to stand by the teams which you root for, then you enter into a social contract which dictates that you should stand by them in the best of times and well....you know the rest of the chorus of that tune. There are several matters to consider which I sense we as a sports obsessed society are not fully aware of. First, we should all see it as part of our responsibility (see: duty) to support teams that are in the same city/state/region as the one in which we pay taxes. This makes sense on several levels and to explain it more fully I think it is best that I outline why the presence of the "bandwagon" fan has necessitated the need for us all to understand our place within the nation of supporters that we call friends, family, comrades and the like.

The Bandwagon Fan: Here is a fan which some of you may commonly refer to as "fair-weather". I like you, despise such a fan in that they make it there business to root for whatever team/college/organization happens to be successful at any given time. I once observed an individual with "bandwagon fan sickness" root for the Oakland raiders in the first half of a Superbowl that they were winning and then turn around and root for the Tampa Bay Buccaneers in the second half of said game when they had overtaken the Raiders. I thought about inviting every-one of us in the room to throttle him but I doubt that it would have done much for his sickness. This particular individual reasoned that because he is from another country he can root for whatever team he chooses....*oh really*...well just please excuse the hell out of all of the many fans who have suffered while their teams went through a number of drafts, playoff heartaches, disappointment, con-tract squabbles....we are talking about growing in a family here, and this sicko wants to walk in after all the work has been done and say that he has played his part. I think not. It is marvelously insulting for such an individual to think that the revelry that comes with waiting for your team to have their opportunity in the winner's circle is theirs to share in with you. There should be some social agree-ment between true blue supporters of a given team, so that there is some means by which a beat down is given for a number of bandwagon fan infractions: a bandwagon fan buys team paraphernalia, then they should be doused in beer and tossed out on the street. A bandwagon fan walks around high fiving fellow fans under false pretenses; they should be socked in the jaw by the biggest chef from the tailgate party. I mean, we are talking about false representation. These bandwagon fans have absolutely no honor and they should be dealt with like the scourge within our sports community that they are.

I am certain that a number of you shared some of the experiences that I had in my youth where I, a youth from a major city (see: New York) had to deal with the presence of "fans" who supported teams from other locales. I grew up a Knicks fan and it both amazed and angered me that in the heart of basketball season in the largest city in the country, I had to hear about the obsession of Chicago Bulls "fans". Further investigation revealed several things about this lot of charlatans. Under close scrutiny, this group often endorsed being fans of the Bulls since birth or shortly after. This of course, is complete nonsense. If these "people" were being honest with themselves and others then they would admit that they became Bulls fans circa 84 A.J. (after Jordan). It is because of the presence of his airness that the Bulls, formerly a terrible professional franchise achieved any level of national notoriety. How dare these individuals try and convince you and me that they had honor as sports fans. I go back to my initial contention about supporting teams located within tax-paying distance. It is like the base of a marriage where you learn to appreciate all of the best and worst of your partner. That is akin to experiencing the highs and lows of supporting your local team. What these accursed bandwagoneers want to do is jump on board of the hottest ticket in town. Understand that there is no way for this brand of foolishness to be tolerated.

Consider that friend who magically appears when you have the money for drinks and other perks. You know somewhere in your mind that when your supply of money runs out then this person is going to disappear like vapor. These bandwagons are no different, they should be dealt with like the treacherous filth that they surely are.

Many of you may be thinking, "should I not have the latitude to root for whatever organization I see fit?" To this I say that you are allowed to root for whoever you choose, but you should look to be criticized for your lack of character in the face of the certain adversity that your teams will face. Why would a person who has been raised in Cleveland want to root for the Cowboys from Dallas? What does an individual from Cleveland who has parts of the cold and Rock n Roll and barbecue and the Dawg Pound and the Tribe in their upbringing need of another team? Look at times with your time as you would times in your life. There are some dark days, hungry times; lean living that you experience as a youth, and quite often your character has been strengthened as a result of these trying experiences. Similarly, your teams had to struggle with young draft picks growing into superstars, potential superstars turning into busts, players retiring and even many of these players exploits being woven into the fabric of the city.

Surely I can venture into the city of Brotherly Love and order a Philly steak sandwich, but the correct way to make these sandwiches, the best places to get them and the occasions on which those culinary delights should be devoured. See Philly knows their steak sandwiches and their night clubs and their schools and their churches and well…once again you get my point. I am familiar with all of these things in my town and you know them in your town…teams birthed from the spirit of our cities should and do receive the same treatment. The unique understanding of our cities and our teams within the borders of those cities is not meant to be taken lightly. You should take it upon yourself to root for your team in the same way you stand up for your cherished relationships, because it is in fact one of your cherished relationships. In the face of our changing and fluid world, there are others questions to be answered in reference to one's allegiance to the teams that serve as members of our families. Such as:

What should be done for someone who lives outside of a major city:

This is a matter which is actually easily resolved. The team which is closest to you geographically is the one which you are likely to have grown up with. Be true and follow that team. There will be occasion for you to venture into the city where the team is located and you will find yourself among many who share your experience. For those who live roughly half way in between two major cities I would recommend that you get a sense of what kind of community you live in and what team is followed more closely. Your sporting community is always the best resource that you will have as you grow as a sports fan. Living outside of a major city is no excuse…you too must join the ranks and fall in.

I live in Fargo, there aren't major sports teams for miles, what do I do?

We live in a society where there are sports on all levels everywhere. There are college towns with college sports everywhere. These are an invaluable resource which makes it possible for those outside of the mainstream to participate. If you wish to become further involved as a supporter of pro sports teams, see above.

I have a wife/husband/boyfriend/girlfriend/significant other, and we root for two different teams, what do I do?

There is no sport in our society where two teams play one another in every game on their schedule so the tension between you and your partner can/should be limited in that regard. If you have a significant other that "talks smack" and enjoys seeing your teams lose as much as they enjoy seeing their own win then you may want to brush up on your own smack talking. If your teams aren't as good as theirs then you must settle for small victories in the form of funny quips, insults and witty banter. If you have children, my suggestion is that you begin influencing them early in their development when it comes to rooting for your teams. Your significant other may try a similar tactic, but things like team apparel, wall paper, team songs and the like can give you an edge.

I lived in one city and moved to another, do I have to switch allegiances

It is all about dedication baby, use your head

I only like watching one sport, do I have to root for all the major sports franchises in my city

I don't believe you have to. Those sports that you adore are a no-brainer when it comes to showing your love, but if you come across a situation where a team from your home is in the playoffs, championship etc., it is your responsibility to show as much support as is humanly possible (see: tolerable).

I am an African-American, am I also required to support sports at HBCUs?

This is a tricky one, but I will try and provide some sort of road map. Quite frankly, sports at HBCUs are terrible. Nonetheless, the brothers and sisters on these teams need the same kind of support that any struggling franchise does. Even if the team itself is not very good, the sheer energy of the crowd can make gladiators out of mortal men (women). Your energy can propel the young men and women on the playing field and you will get more than their all. You should see it as a rare privilege to be able to root for a given HBCU if you have been blessed with the opportunity.

Go out and heckle your local bandwagon, remember to always tailgate when you have the chance to do so, watch, root, cry, drink, eat, sob, whine, jump, embrace, scream and do whatever it takes to get your team up and over the top. Your team needs you.

P.S. GO YANKEES!

REPORTING LIVE

This just in....

Bush is re-elected

The business of being poor and disenfranchised is neglected; maybe the franchises and businesses are busy minding their own businesses

Racial profiling is recorded by the census at an all time high but court cases on police brutality lack credible witnesses

Close to seventy million brown and black bodies living on U.S. soil, but their only piece of that American flag is the red and blue, and you know how those two terrorize your homes and whatever happens to the white...in that flag

Gays want to be married! And all of the conservatives who had sex before marriage and don't pray daily or even love their neighbors and most certainly do not treat others the way that they want to be treated turn out in opposition of the protestors who are standing for gay rights. Political pundits state that our Christian society uses a strict interpretation of the Bible...when it comes to gays

November 2nd comes up and there is enthusiasm among the Democratic Party but DOWN GOES FRAZIER! Experts believe that Democrats are scaring the American public by trying to use government funds to help the less fortunate domestically instead of bombing the less fortunate internationally

Survey says that the two groups with the largest increases in party registration are Black and Latino republican women

Experts say that this increase is due to the fact that Blacks and Latinos are sick of seeing Democrats in their own neighborhoods without jobs going on welfare and taking hard earned money from those who truly deserve it

No word from experts on who these mysterious "really deserve it" types are but we will fill you in as reports become available

Republicans sit back and say "hey the coloreds want a little more cheese on their sandwiches too" and new Black Republicans begin to dance, sing and play basketball to show that they buy the party line. Latino Republicans begin to dance and cook exotic dishes to demonstrate that they too fall in step with the party. Hardline Republicans fear that there is an affirmative action campaign being undertaken within the party and begin to write up legislation before being told that the new faces of color have joined the part voluntarily. More details as they become available.

The independent party issued a statement but absolutely no one heard it. Rumor has it that it had to deal with the deadly stranglehold that the two party system has on American society, but again these reports have not been substantiated, our fact checkers are on the case and we will have that story for you shortly

All of the Black members of the president's cabinet have resigned and many within the party wipe their brows and hold a second victory party and immediately ask several of the parties retired members to come out and take up the vacant positions

The independent party issues a statement, but again there are no details that we can yet sure about it

The five remaining elected Democratic party members in the House and Senate promise that the party will regroup and carefully plan for the next presidential election, that sound of laughter that you are hearing is coming from the Democrats who had just vacated their seats in the House and Senate

An independent, reliable and scientific survey seeks to find out what has brought on the sudden turn away from the Democratic party and the most endorsed idea in the survey was that they (the party) "have no fuckin idea what the people are dealing with day to day". When asked about that statement a high ranking Democrat (a janitor in the White House) states that "I am too rich to worry about what the people think".

Details about the sample have just come out and 100 percent of the sample was independent party members

Breaking story! A popular music mogul creates a voter registration drive among the young in the country that aren't being eaten by the nation itself

A high ranking official after hearing about the drive states "Oh you mean the black guy who put together Ballot Box or Burial Box, someone should tell him that we take the young about as seriously as we take his people…and uh, I don't mean musicians".

The independent party releases a statement on the ballots that 3 percent of the voting public used to support their party. We are still piecing all of the pieces of paper together

Jesse Jackson and Al Sharpton release statements and we have to bring in our interpreters before we can tell you what either of the two leaders said

Breaking sports news: Bush kicks Kerry's ass. TKO round 9. You lose!

Weather: There is a cold front headed our way for the next four years. Dress warm
Did Bush get re-elected?

THIS HAS A TITLE

Truth is
She makes me forget my instinct to think selfishly and has convinced me to pro-
ceed
Into her life helplessly
I need her to see that her happiness is like the picture of me and my sister
The first time that I kissed her
Oh, it's that important to me to know that I at times
Feel that I am in sand that is quick but I am in no hurry or worry
For her voice soothes me savagely and holds me forcefully
Making me want to steal my boy's truck and ride all night
To her doorstep
Pack her things and claim she and her emotions at 2:22 p.m.
I know some would disapprove but I have prayed and told
My mystery god in the sky of my intentions to fall at her feet
And hope that she find me worthy
I pray that I may take all her hurts and worries and make them my own
And sit her upon her throne I have built for her in the very middle of me
She has watched a confused, troubled soul from the hills and has all the while
Obsessed over me though I did not know I was worthy of obsession
If she would just say my name three times
In three rhymes
I would appear behind and reach in her
Appear and reach her inner
I don't even know if my children will even be worthy of calling to her
In a time of need or if I should let her see my emotional bleed
If I scream in disbelief will she heed the sound of my voice?
By choice and join me in this state of emergency with urgency
I have built an altar to her upon which I lay my future
Every pain I have ever felt and even my smile and they have all burned
Turned and returned to me better than when offered
I obsess over the sex we have when she slides her right leg in place

And moans and digs into my shoulders and moans and is wet wet wet
And spins her waist and turns over and I thrust and pull her beautiful brown hair
Damn the hair of the ancestors is strong
And I pull to hold onto the future I see for us just as I...
And now come to my senses and then I...again for 50 years and
Each morning knowing that I have met the one of the most high's favorite
Meant for me
I hope that I can be reincarnated and enjoy her next self for another
Hundred years
But even she could not be as fly as the one I have right now
She need not wrap he hair
For she wraps her thoughts and ways in the robe I gave her last epiphany
And she declared me king and I believed her
I traced the Nile along her spine and found the place where I live
To seek out more of her
My search for and with her has been unending, torturous, joyous
And how I have grown and hope to grow in her my seeds
And prove myself with deeds and with manhood
Provide leads and it has occurred to me that I satisfy
All her needs
She is all that I want as I crawl, face prostrate
To her heel and seek approval
Why does she love me?

...THE REVOLUTION MUST BE....

Approved by your publisher and edited for content so that the intellectual elite can be sure that they won't see your complex work in the hands of the common man

because it is the task of the modern day revolutionary to discuss the problems of the people, the common man and woman, the children, and all those with voices that will not be heard at any volume but the modern day revolutionary must remember to remain at a distance from said groups. This tact is taken so that the mind of the revolutionary freedom fighter will not be clouded with the trivial thoughts of day to day living, they are after all planning the future for us all, having direct contact with us all might compromise their ability to craft verse so beautiful that it brings tears to the eyes of the reader, paints a picture so disturbing that the reader is moved to action, is moved to purchase more works by these intellectuals and start reading and discussion groups about the problems of those low in SES and doomed to live across the tracks and forced to work menial jobs for pay that they cannot possibly hope to raise a family with or have any sense of pride or self actualization with and send their children to school so dreary and poorly staffed that the cycle of poverty should be one of the requisites for children in middle school, middle passage is what that point in their young lives should be referred to as. So once the publisher finishes going over the work and sees that there is just the right amount of anger tempered with rationalization and intellectualism he can then call his associates at any number of publications around the world of literary review and sell his new found glory of a revolutionary writer as "controversial, cutting edge, a voice of change" and try and find a picture for the cover of the revolutionary work where you see a brown hand reaching, reaching for something but you are left to imagine what it is, maybe for another freedom fighter's work. And so the publisher begins to contact his webmaster about including this next author on the webpage and instructs them to put this writer in the same section as the controversial gay and lesbian writers who write about gay and lesbian issues, the controversial conservative political leaning writer that rights about conservative political leaning issues, the Asian and Latino writers who write about Asian and Latino issues and the woman writers who write about women's issues. Once this is done the publisher then seeks a suitable tour schedule for the writer so that enough of the intellectual elite can get their hands on the book on the right bookstore shelves and given to commoners in a slow, methodical manner so as to not overload their senses, they are after all, only human. The newly minted revolutionary's revolutionary must then make a few well timed public appearances and do a smattering of interviews so that their gospel is spread and the intellectual elite can see that they are available from public speaking appearances and lectures at a campus near you. Ivory towers provide a gripping backdrop for the force and power of the revolutionary rant. They provide enough room to set up a table for the writer's works to be sold somewhere in the rear of a given 600 seat lecture hall and the steps leading to the stage provide a long enough journey for said writer to be welcomed to the masses of the university community as a conquering hero. The revolutionary can then get a university appointment like guest lecturer several times a year or they can make themselves available to be contacted by any number of news outlets in the event of a racial emergency where a freedom fighter's expertise is needed to explain the mindset of the people. The cameras are set up in the revolutionaries sprawling home so as to inform the public of their expert standing and they can then begin to expound on any number of ways in which the poor and hopeless are going to behave in response to a given set of circumstances or racially driven incidents in their communities, kind of like a war reporter giving the public the sense of what crosses the mind of an individual on the front lines somewhere on the Southside of their town, the interviews themselves are usually conducted in a whole other city, because as mentioned earlier the revolutionary must have their space in order to fight the good fight. Being on the front lines is for those who are foot soldiers, the selling of the revolution in hardcover and later in paperback is for those with the minds and ability and wherewithal and….

…Granted the stamp of approval in your local coffee house on the two nights a week that are set aside for the sole purpose of the "slam". It is the poetry slam that allows for the broadening, sharing and expanding of revolutionary ideas. It is the wellspring of emotion within the slam crowd coupled with the caffeine buzz that makes all of the difference in the movement. Unlike the world of commercial book publishing, it is in the land of poets that one can get swept over by a tide of revolution so deep that one would take a pen and paper and proclaim as loudly as they can: "I will fight the powers that be, thee will not control me".

Another poet is born and the revolution has another who has joined the hallowed ranks. Even if the work is not the greatest, the point is to have a standard revolutionary name for your pieces, to wear the revolutionary uniform of the day complete with the freedom fighter's messenger bag and your red black and green wristbands. The house band will strike up a tune worthy of a no nonsense revolutionary spirit and mind and give you enough time on stage to light your candles and pump your Black fist up, to be followed by the White and Asian fists that are scattered among the crowd also pumping up the fist. No one will remember precisely what it is you actually said, because the venue is about creative energy and empowerment and stardom. So you want to say the most mundane of things in a rather deep, emotionally scarred way so as to give the impression that your work as a poet and revolutionary is your life. You want to swing your 'locks enough that the crowd swoons with them and flies and flies….You want to close your eyes as you embrace the microphone so as to lead the mass around you to that far off place that you venture when you write and create your masterpieces. You want to leave the stage to the applause and adoration of the crowd who understand how misunderstood you truly are and want nothing more than to make you feel welcome among them and want to make love to your body and your thoughts because you are a revolutionary and they love you and need you to lead and they need you to allow them to follow. But only on Thursdays and Saturdays from 9p.m. to 2a.m.

…Seen through the eyes of the spiritual and religious zealots who assure all those misguided souls that any religion but their own is going to mean the end of all freedoms for the Black man and must be forsaken. They must show you that if you want revolution that you must call yourself by your true name, not the one found in the books that you have been reading all this time but the one that they have found in a book that had been buried for thousands of years, purposely kept out of the possession of the Black man for the sole purpose of keeping his community from rising up or provided for the Black man by one prophet who is more real than any other supposed prophet because they speak of revolt and revolution and taking and owning and living free as a community. The basis for said religion or movement is of no real importance, only take your place in line and call yourself whatever name it is that has been held from you all these many years. No more praying to a mystery god in the sky or worshipping at a Europeans altar or calling one self a slave's name or working for a slave's wages, this part of the revolution is about the ownership of self and taking your place and establishing your own identity…as given to you by this revolutionary spiritual/religious sect.

Being that it is revolution these groups can freely use ideas from other traditions, combine them and give the package to you in a new form…for a contribution of course, because revolutions must be funded by the people who are going to most benefit from them. Some of the practices of the groups will seem familiar, like interpreting the books of religious use for specific purposes and the attacking of other groups, but it is all in the name of freedom and freedom fighters have no time to be apologetic. If there is progress to be named, there a road must be paved. This wing of the revolution may recruit from within the prisons, from the street corners or wherever it is the common man and woman needs to be freed from the chains that have bound them to their current position. Here is where the revolution builds on the old to give you the new?

Do this. Get up and move toward your closest reflective surface. Take both of your index fingers and put them to your temples. Close your eyes and repeat the following five times, "The revolution begins in here".

I WILL NAME THIS LATER

So I am wondering out loud in my head
what
if anything I can do about my lack of focus
several things including she and I occupy my mind's eye
as seconds drip
for the sake of sanity (yours and mine)
I will discuss the details of my tryst as thoroughly
as I am able
I have never discussed she and I because
it didn't occur to me until
a few short minutes ago how much
of an effect knowing/loving/missing her
has had on my life
she often did certainly make my life better
but this may have been for the wrong reasons
that hole she filled I gradually managed to fill on my own
let me admit that I used her
I fed off of what she was and offered
I fully understood that she could almost
never satiate me
and still I allowed her to believe that she could…
I imagine that here in this space of time I
should ask her to forgive me for my selfishness
forgive me for not letting her move into the life of a man
who could have provided the haven that she needed
but only as her friend
she offered me her love and her body and her secrets and I now have knowledge
of these that I did not deserve
on the day that she told me that she had found someone who was
able to see and know all of her without having his needs addressed first
I knew then that she had found what we all search for

the part of me most linked to jealousy and regret felt a certain loss that
I could never be this man or know his place
Or experience his happiness
she is blessed to be loved by a man who is far better for her than me
to her, I apologize for being myself at that most trying of times

...TO ALL THE MASTERS OF ILLUSION

I write you primarily out of admiration for how uncomplicated (is that the word that I am looking for?) that the lot of you have made my walk down this path. Though there are points where our paths veer and bisect, I write to you wherever you may be to ask you for further guidance. It has occurred to a time or two that you struggled with the same self defining issues that my generation of apprentices must deal with. Some of the doubts that we find ourselves confronted with are those that you too had to fend off in order to assume the place that you now have among us. How was it possible in your time when the threats to the completion of your task were so much more overt and thrust at you the minute you left the confines of your home (in some instances drowning out any peace or quiet you could have within your home).

There are heights that you had to scale the take the smallest of steps and I wonder if there was any frustration that entered into this practice. I find myself considering other options at certain times, only to abandon such foolishness later; the voices never really die down though, do they?

I wonder how you were able to pull your way up out of the muck of those schools which are really little more than holding pens with a warden given the task of ushering as many semi-capable bodies through the labyrinth of formal education (considering that there are studies that endorse the idea of there being different methods of learning culturally, one wonders why education is still meted out in a uniform manner). You have indicated to me on more than a single occasion that there was a certain joy that you took in pursuing your studies and much of that pleasure is what balanced the criticism (unfair?) and praise (deserved!) that was heaped upon you during the process. When there were those among us who attacked you for trying to be members of another community, wanting to be less like yourself, less like us. What part of your commitment is it that was questioned? Those before you had always prided themselves on hard work, on wanting their own. When they question how you speak and sound, they fail to understand that duality in speech and presentation has always been a

41

part of your experience. You have always had to put on a certain face in order to convince the King that you are not a threat to him or his safety (even though you reasonably could be one considering that you are offered only scraps to feed yourself with). To be placed in what can be called a school in name only, with your peers having already been given the lesson that there is no room for your brand of mind to succeed, and "teachers" who in many instances were too afraid to teach or who like your peers questioned your aptitude was a sure recipe for cyclical disaster. Such lessons and circumstances had been given to your father and to your father's father.

Somehow you cut a swath through that jungle of doubt and derision and failure at all sides and emerged to take up position closer to the king that the rest around you. He should have rightly been threatened by your dexterous mind and insatiable thirst for progress but it is your very ability to effectively deal with the king and your own people that has allowed you to be where you are. You felt threatened by those who normalized your ability to fail, but you managed to step over the trap they arranged for you. You managed to drain all of the knowledge that you could from your teachers and your schoolbooks and your school district, as limited as the resources were, and trained yourself to want more.

It is because of the steps that you took bravely (audaciously?) at that time that I can now walk the path with confidence because all of the traps are now marked clearly for a discerning eye to see.

The temptation was there for you to forget the face of your fathers and cling to the ways and values of a community that is foreign to you, but you managed to remember to return to us with new knowledge and new plans of actions and new ways to deal with the threats around us. Your tact was to learn first how to survive, then to eventually thrive and live. You decided to take no prisoners and make no exceptions. Such hesitation would have surely led to the downfall of all of your kind. I thank you for standing so firmly. The belief is that the praise which rains down from the mouth of the king and his subjects made you feel as if you were different (better) than those within the community that birthed you. The idea was posited that you began to believe that the praise coming from the king's subjects and their criticism of your community somehow instilled a sense of self-hatred in you. I know better from having been on the path. You hear the way in which you are talked about and realize that the only difference between yourself another member of the fraternity that you were born into is that you made a difficult choice that took you into the teeth of the force which hates you most and he made a choice that drew him into the depths of self-destruction. You realize that you could have been him without less guidance, without the blessings from on high.

How was it first arriving for class and work and being looked at as an experiment? As one who was granted their position by happenstance or the favor of a foolish king? I imagine that it had to be tremendously difficult. Again I sense that doubt had to be a constant companion. Even when you began to advance I am certain that there were those in your community and in others who wanted no part of having to work alongside you. Somehow you managed to restrain your complete frustration and still push forward in pursuit of more. What drove you? When you eventually found your home in the hills and had the authorities stop you from getting there on several fateful nights what thoughts went through your mind? When the king's subjects wanted you to smile for a picture that would be used to show the progress that his kingdom has allowed for your community what kept you from tearing apart at the very middle? When you had to read and see the failures and losses mounting within your community as it dared to push forward and grow what kept your spirits high?

I imagine that it had to be the same strength that I have been granted now. Only you at the time had to dig deeper to access it. It is the strength that the counsel of mothers massages into us when we are mere infants and it is the same strength that a preacher uses to give hope to a bitter and abused community come Sunday morning and it is the same strength that drove your mother and my mother out of bed Monday to Friday to slave for our meals while the women in the community they worked for could simply bark orders and spend the bulk of their time in leisure pursuits. I stand on your shoulders and know that they are so strong now because of the chip that you had to carry back then. I wish there were some way that I could have made your road and journey easier, but that was not your fate. You had to walk it before me and achieve and fall and rise and win and fight and suffer and change so that I could do the same and our sons could do the same after us.

I thank you for you allowing yourself to be changed so that I could learn and in turn be changed. I can carry the burden several more paces because you did so before me. I cannot thank you enough even though many do not see you or what you do (or what you have done).

Many are not able to see that you move among us because of the presence of those who shame you by tying your manhood into violence, the selling of poison to out community, the marketing of a false identity to other communities and an unwillingness to stand up in the presence of the ruler to tell him that scraps are no longer acceptable. So many have joined these ranks that you are no longer seen as even being present among us. The poison doctor who mans the corner is seen as being more present than you are, he who sells his body for labor on the auction block of entertainment is seen as being more present than you are, the breeding, absent buck is seen as being more present than you are, the unemployed apathetic is seen as being more present than you are.

So I must now walk the path knowing that I too, will be forgotten and lost in the shuffle and forced to try and make our community see that I am present and accounted for. The frustration has always mounted, but I must know that the chip that I carry on my shoulder has already been carried by many of you who are even better than me and I just pray and hope and work toward being worthy of walking the path that you set before me someday. Ashe'

THE CORNER COMETH

So I passed the corner just the other evening
looking at the many shades of overpriced headbands stuck to the skulls
of my brothers
while
my overworked inner voice began to ponder…
…"what are they thinking?"
and just before this question went into repeat in my head
the radio they had surrounded like a shrine answered
my question when a clown
also known as a rapper
in just 30 short seconds
murdered an entire record label
sold more drugs than Eckerds and Escobar
and took advantage of some chic so beautiful
that he forgot her name
He capped off this tirade by telling
all of those within within earshot
that "only God can judge me"
which seemed to have a Socratic effect
on the corner listeners
the daps passed around coupled with head nods
were akin to amen's at morning service
my mind wandered off to the first obvious question:
Where do these cats find time to make records
considering that they also run the streets and pimp these ladies for a living
then I considered the question of whether God is fit to judge me?
I mean, any judge that let's these losers influence children and get paid for it
should be thrown off the bench
I see God as one who may judge out of a sense of convenience
how else would you explain that this man
with his plan

which is to sell crafted lies to those he shares skin
and a home with
is rewarded with another day of life
when the late, great Barry White left us here at 58
How can the Klan exist
to enlist more impressionable minds
to hate mine
when I am down here with my people on the front line
looking for life signs
knowing that my people are suffering
buffering our shattered
sense of self with the pride we take
in putting a round ball in a hole
how many nuts we bust
bustin these cats wearing red
because we feel blue
and the only thing that we don't seem to destroy is the white
white like this page
young like my age
misguided like this nigga on stage who made 170
times what he got paid for some middle aged technocrat
in Wisconsin
so he could look you square in your eye
tell you women aint shit and you and your
homegirl toasted that and continued dancing with that cat
over there with ten different names on his back
a Japanese scent maker on his neck
and German car keys in his pocket
but no love for any but himself in his heart
At the very heart of the matter
is the reality that God has let these people prosper
and allowed you and I to struggle
God is not fit to judge me when I consider
My discipline and restraint in the face of this madness
I do not pursue riches
I do not call my women bitches
I do not aim to fit into ignorant niches
but daily this chip on my shoulder itches

more and more
because it is not like me that these like me want to be
but rather like a lost soul and it is unlikely
regardless of what Spike says that we all will wake up
and God has seen fit to weigh us all down with the worst of us
Seeing my brother die…
…I know what that's like
Seeing an abandoned child cry….
…I know what that's like
Seeing a cycle of learned helplessness and wondering why…
…I know what that's like
Being told to forsake my own brown for the bluest eye…
…I know what that's like
God cannot judge me
For I am too God like

DIG IT….

Look around you suckas

Just take one good long look around you suckas and tell me can you dig it!!

Here we are 36 million strong and ain't nobody getting wasted!

Take another look around you suckas!

All of this….all of this everywhere can be yours if you can just take one good look around you!

Look over here!

We have the Chicago Coons

Standing next to the Detroit Darkies

Over there are the Minneapolis Mandingos

Standing side by side with the Brooklyn Blacksox

36 million you suckas, from all over this dustbowl and there aint a single man, woman or child out here getting wasted

The reason why we have all come here today is to discuss the possibilities…the possibilities for us to own this whole damn thing if you can just look, just see what you have around you and dig it suckas

On all sides of us we have the tools to make this thing ours

Over there are representatives of the military, those among us make up a third of the military! We can take it over right now you suckas! We can shut down the army, navy and marines as long as you can look at what I'm putting down and dig it!

right in front of you are our counsel of mothers who have built two generations of us with their hands and their wills and their knowledge and their love and we can make the thrones for them that they deserve in this world

But for too long we have been wasting one another to get control of a few square blocks that bear other people's names

Leaders of all these groups you see around you have been spilling blood and destroying each other for all these generations in order to say that we control something

And what have we got for our troubles you suckas?

A bunch of boxes where are sons lay....children with no fathers...and a few things that we can't afford no way....

And all we would have to do is look around and decide how much of this big old piñata we want to crack open and take...if you can look long enough and dig it! Take a second suckas!....

If we were to take every dollar and cent that we have among every group and gang and crew from all over and pool it then we would by ourselves be one of the ten wealthiest nations in the world you suckas!

We could use that to build these buildings that we have torn down, we could over the soil where we once spilled our blood and we can equip every family here with the means to produce their own goods and clothes and fruit and water and...look around you suckas!

All of this is built on the bones and sweat of your ancestors and you have every right to take their place in the castle you suckas!

For too long I have stood aside and listened to all of you screaming at the top of your lungs about the city and state where you are from, making the borders of these small, cut off islands your "home"...

What about roaming the plains of this entire land, place to place, and running the whole joint you suckas!

We have shown that we can organize a block, a neighborhood, a housing project, but what if we organized each one of us into one big family!

One fist ready to smash anything in our path you suckas!

One hand ready to stroke our own pain and discomfort

One body ready to move and walk, and lay and stand wherever we please around here you suckas!

One group ready to throw that chump and his gang right out of that pale house on Pennsylvania Avenue!

Tearing the whole sucka down and moving the capitol to Harlem or SWATS or Roxbury you suckas!

We can do it all right here, right now if you can look you suckas!

Dig it now and forever more! Dig it for your kids you suckas! Dig it for yourselves you suckas! Dig it for your wives and children you suckas! Dig it for your future! Look, and if you can look then you can see where we can have it all, if you can just look and see you it...look and see it....look...see....it

DOYOUKNOWWHATIM
SAYINDOYOUKNOW
WHATIMEAN

Disclaimer: My effort has always been to do the right thing (usually) and I notice that many women don't see it anyway; I don't know how much good it does to even shave or put on formal clothing or to even buy drinks or try to converse. These ladies are ignoring me anyway, what exactly am I doing wrong here? Trying to understand them, when that brother over there who tells me that there isn't that much to understand. I am going to figure out myself first and save the love that I think I have in me for myself. Maybe dinners and movies will be better with just me (most certainly less expensive. I am beautiful damnit! (at least that is what my mama tells me).

Someone told me that they like ice grills, so I woke up at like 7 every day practicing mine in my mirror making sure it was just right when I hit the block

So I stormed out with my face screwed up like I smelled something rotten and gave love to the first sister I spotted

I stopped in front of her and loudly proclaimed "holla"

She gave me a negative appraisal and kept it moving. I continued on to class and while there had a eureka moment

Damnit! It's the clothes. That old backpack, bargain basement underground B-Boy look don't get love out here

So I took my last 40 bucks and went to Modell's and picked up a replica (throwbacks cost a bit much, now don't they?)

I came out the next morning and spotted another sister, put my ice grill firmly on and instructed her to "holla at your boy"

Grabbed my crotch and asked "What's really good with you?"

She walked past me and left me to ponder my next move to go from invisible man to Super thug, the unstoppable lover

I listened to every CD I could find to get a better sense of how to approach women and memorized as much as I could

It occurred to me that I have a girlfriend but part of being a thug is having your girl on one hand and on the other is your down ass chic

Plus my girl is too plain man, she don't be knowing the names of any of those drinks when I ask her

She would rather have me as I am, which means no love for me

Thugs be having chics that touch other women, don't I some troi action, Shouldn't I have a dime in my whip….as soon as I get a whip

No more average chics for me man, you have to spend time with them and dimes don't mind if you hit the block

Plus you get love from these cats if your girl is a dime

My boy told me the other day that my girl is bringing down my average. What happens when I blow, is she gonna step and sweat me correctly?

Why should I ignore all the ass if it is there, and she likes running her mouth, dimes aint on that B.S. and maybe I should just date me for a while because it seems that only I can look at life and appreciate it with me, plus I like titties and I can't talk to my girl about liking titties and dimes don't mind if you talk about titties but dimes didn't seem to know my name on the block till my mama said I was in grad school and then I had cookies made for me and two dinner invitations but these cats on the corner still get all this love and haven't I done enough that I should be the man now and why can't my girl, or those dimes, or these others see me, what's wrong with me, why don't they love me?

TO MY PEERS ON
PRETENTIOUSNESS pt 2

It is our shared culture and experience which has made the breadth of our creative expressions so tremendously influential. The unique standing of a community in an occupied land and held in mental and spiritual hostage has caused many others to look at the creations of this special people as a gift. The question must first be, how can one group which has suffered and had to strive for so long have the energy, freedom and wherewithal to erect structures to document what their experience has been. How can this community produce volumes of literary works, draw likenesses and celebrate in song when they have for the balance of their experience been under siege.

Quite simply it is this very same threat in the proverbial air which has directed this community to create. If not for the opportunity and space that creation provides, then madness and despair would surely set in and overwhelm the mass. The feelings of helplessness and hopelessness would surely push a community already on the brink closer to the edge that they have already been accustomed to living on.

It is the culture of creation and expression that has allowed a community that have had their entire experience marginalized and discounted to tell the entire world around them that they are here and do live and love and hurt and cry and want and long for and obsess over and destroy and rebuild and learn and teach and console and laugh at and with each other.

In our dance and song and rap and instrumentation and preaching and painting is the very heart of our unique take on the human condition. In addition to the standing problems that come with being born man (woman, child) are the problems that a man within this community must face when trying to earn a living, dealing with authorities, supporting his women and children and demanding respect in the world. A woman within this community has the same problems and additionally must face a patriarchal society, and try and heal the often broken and bloodied body of her husbands, sons, nephews, uncles and all the men in her community who have been a threat, while trying to keep from also being seen as a threat by men both in and outside of her

All of these matters converge in culture which includes a salt and pepper combination with schooling, neighborhood, society, money, sexuality and gender to provide the rich wellspring that creative energy within this community comes from.

Even with all of the experiences that we share that give us this special insight into humanity, there seems to be a denial of parts of these experiences. In much of what we do, there are those high minded individuals among us who refuse to acknowledge some of our creations whether rightly or wrongly.

I for my part, try to look into the body of creations which have chronicled my (our) experience and have been both encouraged and disturbed, sometimes at the hands of the same work. Dealing with and sharing these experiences with others is what has often brought out many of my negative feelings while unearthing treasures and fools gold alike.

I have tried to go out with friends and enjoy many of the films from within the diaspora and I find that the conversations around many of these works has colored my opinion of them. Many of my friends, and quite likely some of yours, compare a film from Afro-Cuba or Afro-Brazil with reverence. I am never totally certain why, but many of the films that have been developed by American urban filmmakers are taken quite lightly. A creative product, regardless of its origin should be taken on its merits, but far too many of us want to remain one step ahead of our peers, buying the idea that knowing about a Spike Lee or the Hughes brothers is a joke. They want their films with subtitles so that they wave their flag of knowledge in front of us all in anticipation of a salute.

I will be the first to admit that many of the Black comedies (see: any of the Friday movies or a Soul Plane) are complete foolishness in my book. Many of the problems that we have in the community at large are ridiculed in these films, usually in embarrassing ways. We have always, as a community, been able to laugh at ourselves but are these films really a testament to that or more a selling of the Black identity as little more than a minstrel.

I won't support that kind of a creation because of how poorly informed it tends to be. When would you expect to see Richard Pryor or Redd Foxx, who were some of our most adept social commentators and comedians, in a film of that caliber? The product comes out and tends to be the same, but do you really want to forsake all of what may be out there, effectively throwing out the baby with the bathwater?

Such conversations are had among peers regularly and not just about movies, but about art, music and the like. A picture of a Black church scene is almost entirely forgotten about when the conversation turns to a Monet or a Dali. Why would I not look at Justin Bua's interpretation of a DJ's life as art?

The fact is that we have allowed pretentiousness to color our wants and likes. We go to pains to hide this pretentiousness in beeswax and shea butter, but it eventually finds its way to the surface. We refuse to listen to this particular music because it isn't among the "classics", and why exactly is "Criminal Minded" by Boogie Down Productions not a classic? And why do we sit in a multibillion dollar coffeehouse sipping overpriced lattes talking about what we need to do to make progress when we haven't taken the time to look at the mirror that all of our current creations hold up to our community.

These creations tell the story of where we are and thus inform what progress we should try to make. If we are not familiar with them then there is no way to say definitively what the next step should be. What does urban fiction say about the state of Black relationships and the Black family? What do gospel plays say about our religious and spiritual standing in the world? What obstacles do Black dancers, sculptors and painters face in sharing their respective visions with the world?

If we are too obsessed with measuring these against the majority, then we are often doomed to miss the happiness and strength that our people pour into what they create, and that, has indeed happened. We are only prepared to give kudos to an artist that has been awarded by the majority first. We want creators that have been awarded credentials by European institutions even if their art is fed directly by our community.

At what point are we ready to love what it is we create, choose carefully how we allow our experience to be marketed and select our own pioneers in storytelling, painting, dancing and the like? My fear is that we will continue to look away from what we have at home out of a sense of shame and embarrassment. We hate the sound of the South in our voices, the spread of our mouths, the gleam of our skin and the honey in our laugh. If we returned home for a time, maybe then we could see the very beauty that others obsess over in the artifacts of our existence.

VIGILANCE IN AFTERTHOUGHT

So I believed that I had a concept of the ideal woman for me when I was 12
And it changed again at 16 and once more at 20
But even she could not be that ideal because every time I see her
I remind her that she doesn't sound like you, she doesn't look like you
She isn't fiery and let's be honest
She cooks entirely too much
So an ideal is really just a sad conception
That doesn't by necessity measure up to reality
Lucky for me I am a cynic or I would not have been braced for the fall
So ideally I never bothered to think about my emotions
And how wrapped up in mine you have become,
Inescapably so
Like I have grown with you and shed a skin
Can you hear me thinking about you?
Picturing you not too tall, in front of me
Needing me to scribble my hieroglyph
Down the small of your back
Needing me to be even more humble
To quiet my racing thought long enough to hear the language
That you and I speak
I realize I cannot walk away
I cannot be passive with the fight that commences between
I that is in we and I that is in the world
Could you really mean me no harm?
Then how am I so driven at times in your company and moved to ease
In other instances
What am I prattling on about
These things you knew already.

NORTHBOUND-SOUTHBOUND

9:18 a.m.

I take this train every day, Northbound before school so that I can get to my part time position at Lennox Mall. I am certain that I have never seen this queen that I now stare at, shamelessly, but I think that she is familiar to me. I have met her somewhere...

The sister is filling the train car with her energy and maybe she doesn't understand how it is wafting through the tangle of people positioned between her and me and drawing me undivided...

I have seen her style of dress before, and I have noticed that kind of beauty, but never have I been blessed to see this combination forced together from birth on one being, one of God's children, she is not smiling, but I can see how the light of her skin must play when she does smile and how can I steal one of her looks my way?

Her head is wrapped in an African style that I have seen many of the sister's at school wearing and it feels almost as if I have never seen it before. Who are her parents and what is she doing here? She should be near me, though she doesn't know me and why can't I just simply call out to her and tell her that I look forward to the experience of her loving me, because I am certain that that is what she is intended to do.

9:21 a.m.

I notice that this brother is staring at me from about 15 feet away in the car and where I would usually be uncomfortable with such a stare, I sense that he means me no harm. I have already glanced at his beauty and I can see that he has much to offer, he is saying much of it with those wonderful eyes of his. I usually sit farther back on the Northbound train on my way to Arts Center, but I see that fate had a greater plan today. Good thing I lotioned my feet with these sandals I am wearing, because he is taking in all of me at his leisure. We haven't said a word to one another, but I could truly do this all day.

9:25 a.m.

She just glanced over here. The smallest hint of a smile played across her river of lips and I readied to mouth a hello before she returned her attention to the book she has in her lap.

I usually write pieces on this ride, but there is no chance that I am going to be able to concentrate with this goddess in front of me….

…Three more stops

9:28 a.m.

Maybe I should just approach him. It is clear now that he is not going to give up staring at me and I just hope that I am not blushing or flushed. He appears to be trying to write something…what kind of a writer is he? He has on glasses and they add character to what looks to be an already wise face, he is blessed with what the elders call an old soul

I wonder what his sons will look like? Will he stare this intently at his sleeping daughters?

No, I will not take him off of the hook, if he has something to say, he must wind through this people traffic and say it, I am eager to hear his voice….

9:31 a.m.

My legs are moving and I still can't figure out what I going to say once I get over to her.

Returning to my seat is not an option since a young woman occupied it the moment that I vacated it. I imagine that the powers that be are forcing my hand. What should I say; I mean I have never really approached a woman this gorgeous before in my life. The very air around her testifies to how much in love with her any man should be

Four steps, three steps, two steps…..“Hello”

10:15 a.m.

It turns out that his name is Josiah and it is a name that has a sense of regality to it and fits him quite well. It turns out that he is a psychology student and wants to open up a community based practice. Something about him told me that he was a healer. I am on my way to work now and I can't get his smell and touch of his hand off of my mind. I can picture him discussing world events or moving chess pieces or….well, let's just say that I am impressed. I can't wait until I see my great brown obsession once more. Just sharing a few minutes with him was my pleasure.

10:23 a.m.

She and I spoke for sometime and it was indeed as if we knew one another from a time that we each enjoyed somewhere in our past. She gave me that smile and it was more than I as a mortal man was prepared to handle. I fully believe that I have met the mother of my children and she is the descendant of a long line of priestesses from a village in West Africa. The energy that she passed on to me in her presence will carry me through my week. I hope to spend the entire weekend with her, and I hope further that she is my life partner and the mother of my children. I honestly don't know whether I could rightly handle meeting another like this queen again.

THE INDICTMENT

You stand accused
I accuse you of various crimes of which you are a repeat offender
There is no sense in pleading, you have been found guilty on all counts
I will however explain, since you are entitled to due process

For the first charge you stand accused of assuming a non-caring, oblivious and ignorant stance in the face of despair and death and poverty and hopelessness and voicelessness for those not born to look like you, then taking a stance of moral relativism, heterosexism and hypocrisy against all those who dare not think like you

You are accused of stereotyping me and my brethren as Negro X and painting us with the same broad brush, not only in your thought and conversation, but in your media and social policy, all of which acknowledges my faults ad naseum but blanks out, whites out and removes my strengths in a Ralph Waldo Ellison like fashion and you wonder why one in that position, screaming at the top of their lungs from within a cage of tenements and crowded decay with a lack of "education" as a padlock and their own washed brain for a warden would rename themselves in the crossest of ways...

...But I know what they are thinking and I see how these screams resonate so loudly with your oh so impressionable and according to you innocent co defendants that we will heretofore refer to as your children. No, they weren't killing themselves and doing drugs and raping and cursing and lying before they began to idolize men who look like me, no not your progeny, the apple of your eye who is apparently dragged kicking and screaming to that concert, to that music outlet and to that side of town, let you tell it. You call that man and I one, yet, he and I are not, but different points on a single continuum, one shaken by manipulation and oppression, and too many other things to list here in these proceedings.

You feel threatened by an ambitious me and at what point do you realize that I am your problem I cannot just sail away to another continent or scrub my skin or voice away, and you and I are sentenced to life.

Next is you

And you are charged with misrepresenting, blaspheming and above all else forgetting your responsibilities to yourself and to the integrity of the honor guard which we were both born into. You have forgotten your place and on the one hand painted me/you as childish, impulsive and unintelligent and on the other as lacking in direction and drive. For this I recommend the swiftest and most immediate punishment.

You are to stare at the mirror that is my soul and do so until you claim the shame and become again what I/we/you have always been. Until you arm yourself with knowledge and community and commitment and concern for your mothers and sisters who will eventually be wives and elder mothers, until you heed the voice of your father and seek out his counsel your body will remain incarcerated

I offer you the opportunity to be set free from the lockdown of the hood with no neighbors and closed mindedness, I will tell you how to avoid the CO's in the form of apathetic leaders and I will place a bullhorn to your lips and give you the opportunity to free Bunche and Wright and allow you to embrace your children/wife/me, your brother

Until that time, you are guilty.

And you

You stand accused of giving up on your family/loved ones/me at the point at which you are most needed and submerged yourself in a world and shell of superficiality and selfishness that has caused the world around to see you as something that you are not now and never have been.

You are not promiscuous and superficial and unsupportive and hypercritical, are you? Not from what my previous evidence suggests to me. You are the backbone of your tribe, the most resilient of all people, but you have committed the crime of making the wise, ambitious, humble and spiritual among your brethren feel ostracized, unimportant and doubtful about what he/I means to you.

This to be sure, is unforgivable.

You are further accused of impersonating and accepting what the world, just a few steps off of your porch, would say is you. I however, understand and know you to be strong, moral, intelligent, committed and focused. Not lascivious and loose, not angry and pessimistic, but you have contributed to the aforementioned crimes and thus are guilty

You have the opportunity to be set free, to embrace your family as we are, not a trumped up, fallacious version, but the actual. To raise your daughters without bitterness, to instill trust in your sons and rely on I/we, your brothers.

It is for you that this sentence is reached; you will from now on love yourself and I/we, your family and never return to these chambers.

I need you to understand that there is no room here to send you away, you will have to learn to live rightly and righteously.

We are adjourned.

NEWS AT 11

The U.S. is at war with Afghanistan and Iraq!

When asked to comment on the objectives of the military actions a high ranking department of defense official simply stated "Those bastards are bad Christians, and that we will not allow, we will learn em. Those towels on their heads are affecting the economy!"

This just in, also on the war agenda for the U.S. are Canada (because of their bacon), France (suing the U.S. over the use of "freedom fries" over French fries) and the Dakotas as it has been established that North and South Dakota may not actually be states and are harboring large numbers of Democrats.

Sources nationwide report that Black greek letter organizations are under investigation amidst rumors of several members being terrorists. A White House official stated, "Have you seen those dances, clearly they are linked to some unknown religious sect and where exactly are all those dues they supposedly pay going. Yep, you guessed it, weapons of mass destruction. We hear that they have parties in order to raise money for their terrorist brethren, we will put a stop to this mess right now."

Representatives from several black greek letter organizations upon being reached for comment could be heard barking and making other unidentifiable sounds and hand gestures.

The CIA indicates that these are clearly terrorist signs and Black college students have been brought in to decipher the messages

The Independent party issues a statement saying "we have no idea who in the hell these blacks or greeks are, but we do want them to know that they have a place in the Independent party".

Breaking news!

Jesse Jackson and the Rainbow Coalition issue a statement, but it arrived too late for it to make it onto the air, in a related story Julian Bond and the NAACP issue the following statement, "Jesse is still alive?"

This just in, parents in several urban centers are ecstatic about the progress made with the no child left behind act. With all of the students that crowded the best schools in every city, making those schools failing schools, the 18 students left in the worst schools in every city were able to get individual attention and are now the best students in their respective cities. No word on what the fate of the former best, now worst schools will be.

A ranking Department of Education official gloats "see, that was our plan all along, isolate the bad students in one place, get the others some learning, and off to college with em".

A high ranking White House official asks "What exactly is this no child left behind thing?"

The Independent party issued the following statement, "All of those kids who have been left behind have a place in the Independent party".

Breaking news: Social security in jeopardy, may be defunct by 2037, leaving millions with no benefits after retirement

An influential politician states "hey, it isn't a problem, just get rich quick, and you will be okay in your old age."

Sources report that the entire Republican party nods in unison

The Congressional Black Caucus discusses the future of Black politicians running for the highest offices nationally and can't come to a consensus on who could run for president

Jesse Jackson who was not in attendance states that "I don't want it to be that Powell boy and the person ought to be able to sing the theme to Good Times, keep hope alive".

The Congressional Black Caucus issues the following statement, "Now you know why Jesse wasn't here, man".

The Independent party issues a statement "There is a place for Jesse Jackson in the Independent party".

Bush got re-elected?

VAPOR

This piece that I am reading tonight is not going to
be about the revolution as you may want to call it
but it will revolve around how my thoughts revolve around how I can
make her every second happier than the one before it
her being Isabo and that my coffee house warriors
is a fitting name for a revolutionary
seeing as she now stands just within a pinch of my thoughts
about my future and they tend to revolve around
her place in that future
her being Isabo, the same Isabo you and I went round and round about earlier
she, the revolutionary
And as such she, like yourselves my coffeehouse mates
has made many parts of the revolution vogue
notice the beautiful smile and lovely cheeks with the light of the sun
revolving around them
and because of her the freckled negroes with car coats and toe rings
can now put on their I am the Dream shirts and pump their oddly
shaded fists while rocking to the Youngbloodz, but I digress
this piece is about her revolution from girl to woman and how much milk
revolves in and out of her bosom
to make it so full when before it was....
Counterrevolutionary
and the curve of all that backside is one full revolution
and if we had panthers like her I would have waged love and not war
my thoughts revolve around this sharp revolutionary and her bad self
let me turn to my next piece which revolves around money and honor
and afros and Egyptian musk and Donnie Hathaway and tantra and caramel
apple cider
and I am spent, but can always turn to her huh huh huh huh
and the revolution between her thighs
the sight of me in her eyes

the savannah in her walk
the honey brown in her talk
and pardon me and her
her being Isabo, the revolutionary
we have a revolution to plan against bad relationships and
so called divine minds that advocate lying on stage
but who will lecture you for eating a ham and cheese sandwich
Run for cover, cuz her thighs are out
her two round tasty spies are out
and I am standing behind her pumping gas into
the war machine one stroke at a time
It's On!!!!!!

THE WRITING IS ON YOUR FALL

Okay, so I am watching football and an interesting thought occurs to me: It is far cooler to be a writer than it is to be an athlete. And yes, I do mean this seriously. It confused me at first, but there is a type of method to this madness. To start with, authors, novelists, essayists and writers can be closer to their public than can a football player. No helmet, no pads, no private locker room or such. Just a table at a bookstore. If you ask me, it is this brand of intimacy which makes the practice or writing such a joy for those who do it.

Now, I already dropped this idea on a few acquaintances and after the laughter and the realization that I was serious, they proceeded to give several reasons why being an athlete is supposedly "cooler" than being a writer. Athletes make millions of dollars, have fame and they have the hottest girlfriends and groupies.

Point taken, but again I assure you that being a writer has more of a coolness factor to it than all of the above mentioned. First, writers record the history of our experiences and more often than not, it is done out of some sense of love for the craft. Occasionally, a Stephen King is given birth to and he is indeed wealthier than Pharaoh. Granted there are only a handful of writers in his class financially, but a few trumps none.

Next, writers also have adoring fans that are truly committed. I conceded that these fans do not paint themselves or wear a jersey with an author's name on it, but they do invest in the works of authors in addition to attending lectures and book signings.

For the benefit of fans of writers, there is a saving of finances and a better bang for one's buck than is offered by athletics. One of my aforementioned acquaintances asked me if I was on any controlled substances when I made the above statement to them, but I assure you that I am not. A ticket to an NFL game can run into 60 or so dollars in the highest reaches of a given stadium. If you intend to take a friend of family to this event you can get a sense of how costly such a proposition can be.

Observe how writers look out for their fans. A hardcover copy of a book may run you in the range of 25–30 dollars and will provide more than three or so hours worth of entertainment. There is very little writer paraphernalia for a fan to have to invest in, so there is an instant savings there and as long as one has the book already in hand, then book signings tend to be arranged at no further cost. Now, who would you support?

Next you have girlfriends and groupies. Many athletes take it upon themselves to acquire the latest trophy (model, actress), whatever the order of the day demands. They are beautiful and probably seem like a lot of fun, but athletes have to then suffer the increased media scrutiny, law suits, paternity suits, stalking etc.

Writers very rarely have this issue, though I would argue that our girlfriends and groupies bring more to the table in the way of quality. They have already shown that they can take the time to understand and dissect books and this is likely a function of a beautiful personality that has a great deal of mystery, depth and even a little spice mixed in.

People will tell you that ladies dig athletes, and I submit that ladies would dig intelligent writers belting out a classic if they were given half a chance. Writers tend to be content with whatever money, fame and adoration comes with the love that they feel for their craft. I would figure that it has to be very cool to be a Lawrence Block and be able to shop at your local mall without being harassed for autographs and pictures and what not upon sitting down for a meal.

Being a writer is cool in that you can't be preoccupied with being cool, no one really thinks that you are and this obliviousness is some of what makes it cool. You have to love writers because even if you don't, writers love writing, and that my friend is quite chilly.

HOPELESS

I wouldn't say that I am a hopeless romantic
but I am hopeless
there is no hope for me
when I
an intellectual
a discretion doctorate,
find myself reading intensely
and then drifting off into my river of you thoughts
going with the flow cannot accurately describe this kind of
daydreaming wherein I can obsess at my leisure
about the ginger over brown of her skin
and my eyes fall out of focus because she has trapped me
in her sea of flesh
maybe she did so deliberately
I can smile as she paws at herself in the mirror for
she doesn't realize that she is in fact vain
I would crawl to her and bite her earlobe and whisper that she is shaped
more like a woman now than at any other point when I have known her
if I could I would run a hot bath and lay her down in it and just worship
her person in much the same way as the hot droplets
I would stroke her mane and say a quiet prayer on behalf of our union
I would be upfront with her about my private man moments
admitting to her that she has forced her way into my fantasies
when I am pleasing myself she now often enters my mind
writhing against and holding me
My fantasy women have gotten jealous of her presence
I would rub her body until my hands ached, hands on oil
oil and touch speak to passion and the slightest touch from her brings that out
I should be concentrating on learning, but my mind is venturing off to her
walking toward and away from me
this woman has given me a reason to strive with just her being

her body, her spirit, her mind
I must admit to this sister that I did not know where to begin
all three reduce me to a needy, anxious being
I want her sex until it aches for her to move away from me
until her daily functioning is compromised by thoughts of loving
until she whispers sweet nothings and jumps up and makes a pastrami sandwich
because her man needs his strength
I want her to be addicted to me, to look at me in a new way every time
to have trouble breathing and speaking, to scheme and produce new ways
of seducing me
I want her body before me with no pride, begging me
it is true that I am hopeless
because I am watching time wind down and up as I desire her doing what she does
to my mind and body and spirit and happiness again.

3rd *FLOOR APARTMENT*

Her apartment was on the third floor and she went to this place called the buzz one night where she heard there would be a good time waiting. The place was dark, but he was off to the side and his skin was light enough that she could see. So was what she took to be a look of arrogance on his youngish face. He looked over and saw her dancing by herself and thought all at once that she looked more Asian than African. More cute than beautiful. The songs slipped as they danced for a while, realizing that neither had any plans of changing partners. He stepped away and kept looking back and she took said look as an invitation to let her gaze follow him. He returned. They continued. Time slipped and he and his friends decided it was time to leave. Neither he nor she had paper or pen handy and dilemma emerged. Music loud, he chooses to shout number in her ear and asks her to remember it. He gets home four days later and is surprised to find that she has called, to remind him she says, the little Asian looking one. He didn't forget. They talk and talk and talk and create a space for just the two of them in it.

Her apartment was on the third floor and she went to see him on 2/14/98 with a gift in a can the gift of herself. He plays music and they talk and laugh and touch and kiss and touch and kiss and touch and kiss. He calls it the most beautiful night he has ever had, she agrees. They touch and kiss and touch and kiss and the morning did eventually come. His past began to creep in with the sun...

Her apartment was on the third floor and he did his usual, called before coming, walked the 3 blocks to her place at a brisk pace and called once up to her window. She would put final he liked so much. She would come down and walk him up. The both of them giddy, happy at ease and trying not to appear too open, thought they were. He would open her door as any young urban gentleman would and would peek at her backyard, which wasn't the best part of her but was more than suitable, nonetheless. Her roommate would always leave so as to avoid getting drowned in their stifling overaffection. This couple is what we all in some way want to be.

The Duke-North Carolina game in Chapel Hill was already under way and he asked her if she would mind if he watched some of it. She agreed, but cursed in the back of her mind because she had no intentions of letting him watch the game until its conclusion. Ten minutes passed. Fifteen minutes passed. At sixteen minutes, thirty seconds she grabbed her notebook and straddled him with her arms around his neck and the book behind his head. He protested of course, "Baby, the game". She replied, "Go ahead I am just reading some notes I hope I'm not distracting you". He looked down and noticed the top she was wearing and she heard the TV go off. In surprise she spun around to see if her sense were failing her and felt his hands sliding and warm breath on her neck. She made as if she were trying to read more, but ended up reading the same line 5 times and simply quit, pushed him back and undid his buttons with her teeth. His hands were still beautiful from the cuticle oil that she had applied a week before and they were a perfect brown and brown combination as a couple and they loved and to this day he still doesn't remember what the score of that game ended up being.

...TO OUR MOTHERS

There is no one who we need more than you and it is with your amazing direction that most of us have navigated these troubled waters. Somehow many of you have managed to perform the task of man/woman and have done so without letting any of the strain effect the beauty that God gave you. Allow me to apologize on behalf of those of my kind who have refused to stand beside you, beside us in your/our time of need and I want you to understand that our troubles as a community are not your failures. Difficulty was cooked into the recipe of our lives some time ago, it is a wonder that you have kept us alive this long, it has to be the force of your will.

Among us there are many who need you even upon leaving your home, because we know that you have somehow confronted the world as a sister and a woman and have managed to live and love even after enduring disappointments and acquiring scars. Those same scars are a map of where our people have come from and gone to under your guidance. It is your voice that we hear in our heads when the doubt tries to creep in. It is your smile that makes taking a chance on venturing past our gates possible.

I am afraid for myself in that one day I will be married to the mother of my children and I will then have the responsibility of caring for, loving and protecting one of you, I don't always believe that I will ever be prepared for such a task. I do however; accept that it will fall to me in time with a renewed sense of pride.

I know that you see all of the bricks that our people represent that have been taken from the foundation of our community and you have still somehow managed to move our children through schools, steered many away from the perils of our lives and moved them into successful adult lives of their own. Each time I go to applaud you for the work that you have done, you sternly remind me that your task isn't done. You indicate to me that too many of our sons and daughters are still locked away somewhere being anything but rehabilitated and you remind me that our children are under siege every day but some of our other children. You force me to look upon the cannibalism in our community that you have fought off tooth and nail, and more often than not, you have won. I can see some of the toll that this fight has taken on you and I still have to marvel at how beautifully you carry this great weight and even go so far as to hide it under those wonderful hats on Sunday and in those big purses you carry and how you even dance and sing all of those troubles away. You carry them for us, and you protect us from them with all of the strength of your character.

I know that we don't make your life any easier and I apologize for us all, your ability to shield us from everything that wants to destroy us has caused us to be lax and careless. At some point, there will be a time for you to be able to take care of yourself, because you have spent far too long holding us up on your own. Mother, I love and dedicate my life to you. There isn't a strong enough word for thank you in any language to express the gratitude I have for what you have done for all of us

HATRED WRITTEN IN MESPEAK 1

When I read my pieces…works of art…poetry I speak in this voice
That is nothing like my own though I imagine that it is the voice
That I should speak in cause we all do that when we read and write
So vaguely and abstractly that only those with a third eye may get
What we say
And it is clear that all those that I break bread with and even those that walk by
daily on any street
Have the two eyes that they view the world with
And if my poetry, masterpiece, work of art arouses
Interest in only your third eye then it stands to reason
That I don't write work for the masses but rather for the few whom
Like me understand misunderstoodness and are not vain or
Cliquish
No, I am a poet, the world most socially social reporter
and if you don't get my version of the news
then I would recommend that you change the channel because
your mind is not divine
but I have this poem like
Baby
Can I creep in at night and trap every breath you breathe while sleeping
Then release it only to hear you when I am not near you
And take this sharpened moment with you in it and carve just an outline of you
on my mind
I would give a thousand lifetimes just to see
The look of love in the eyes of that crowd
And the groupies, oh, the groupies
I would need a thousand lifetimes just to create more clever ways
To lose them in my deepness, pain and fragility
And to bed them all and use that as fuel for my work

And inspiration
And to bring them the word for I am a poet
Reciting
Writing
Giving and changing meaning
And I hate myself for it.

ASK YOURSELF:
THE ATHEIST

God is an atheist. Without question. Whatever definition you cross to suit your idea of an atheist is exactly what god is. This romanticized, sentimental, thoughtful picture of god has been created by the transparent insecurities of man.

Now, man was obviously created in god's image, but god manifested things like death, laws, disease and poverty to keep us in our place...or rather to give himself a feeling of superiority. God literally created man as a vehicle to feel good about himself. He after all, had nothing to compare himself with and thus created creatures with his imperfections and weaknesses and then commenced to turn them loose in an imperfect playpen (earth). God then took a step back and saw the real potential in his creation...for entertainment.

Many believe that we (man) were placed here to praise god, they point to any number of texts to substantiate this belief. Consider that thought for a second. Does a civil engineer want to be praised by a suspension bridge? Does a composer seek applause from his latest sonnet? I would say absolutely not. They want to step back and admire their work when and how they wish. God is no different

He wants to see what this toy called man will crash into when wound up and allowed to run. If you look about in earnest, you will see that we are at times quite interesting and in other instances so very dull. I believe that god finds atheists to be the most interesting of our kind.

They, after all, behave in much the same way as he. The atheist walks about and denounces morality and has very little use for religion and spirituality. He/She creates their own moral code and as a group, they are firmly unapologetic about this. The atheist is largely their own judge, jury and executioner. Now observe god, he didn't wait for any moral standard to be established, he simply stated that I am absolutely right and anything in opposition of what I have established as right is wrong.

God provided each being with a five card hand and sat them down to this winner take all poker game that we have elected to refer to as life. Some people were provided with a flush, others two pair and others were provided with absolutely nothing in their hand. He watches in amusement as we ask repeatedly of him, the dealer, for a better hand. This asking has taken the form of prayers. You can ask every game if you wish, but god may be a smug enough dealer that he can give the impression that he is not listening. He may give you a better hand in order to make things within the game a bit more interesting.

God was bored before he placed us here. He observed us in much the same way as we watch any competitive match or battle for survival in earth's natural environments. Here before you is the ultimate gladiatorial coliseum with god as the chanting mob. God likely finds it humorous that you would turn to him in the midst of a battle and cry out for help. Really, he is occupied with the outcome…winners and losers, in much the same way that we are.

We idolize our gladiators because they represent our standing in the face of our creator. See, god never saw himself as something that had to have praise and adoration. If he did truly feel so, then why would he demand said praise and the like. The truly great never question their greatness, they simply assume it.

Put another way, god has a god complex. He does not truly see himself as fit to be the master of all creation. If he did, there would have been no need for the creation of angels, who are little more than yes men. Once the company of angels became mundane, get created the less predictable being of man.

Soon our own insecurities grew so that we had to create this idea of a loving god to make existence bearable. Believe that god finds this idea somewhat funny. God tunes into our soap opera every day to see what will happen next. He finds characters like Gandhi quite interesting. Oscar worthy. See they unpredictably break the monotony. Most of us mention his name so much that he is forced to reflect upon himself and his shortcomings.

Our expectations are unrealistically high and god feels like a failure when he cannot reach them. Types like Lennon, Shaka and Roosevelt take the spotlight off of him and put it back on us to whom he needs to feel superior.

Atheists serve as a type of reality check and psychotherapist for god. They tell him in essence that he is of no consequence and go so far as to hold up man as proof of the imperfection in the idea of a supreme being. They scoff at the idea of love and compassion being concepts given to us being an almighty being because they see both of these being so devoid in much of man. A look at the makeup of man created in god's image would reveal pettiness, greed, envy, short sightedness, and pig headedness.

It is atheists who boldly state that if our concept of the most high is supposed to be god then they would rather have no god at all. A further look would show that an all powerful being allows many things in our world and lives, including crime, disease, racism, sexism, genocide and a number of other evils, which run rampant without a check.

There has to be some reason why these things continue to go on, and I would submit that they allow for a level of entertainment in what can at times grow to be a very quiet world. Atheists acknowledge that with all that we have taking place around that god is absent. This absence is the same as being non-existent.

God is relieved of certain responsibilities and obligations as a result of this. He will not always be expected to find cures or feed the hungry or educate or answer prayers. He through atheists is free to be a slacker of sorts. Bains of the human existence can go on for a time; god can do what little he chooses or is capable of doing about them and then watch as we trip over ourselves to offer praise for what little has been done.

The vehicle of the world is allowed to crash and we are thankful to god for salvaging a tire. It would stand to reason that a better tact is to keep the vehicle from crashing and causing such destruction to begin with. Maybe there is nothing that god can actually do to prevent it. His creation has possibly outgrown him.

God is an atheist. He has no real belief in himself.

0-595-33947-6

www.ingramcontent.com/pod-product-compliance
Lightning Source LLC
Chambersburg PA
CBHW031302280526
45784CB00004B/1957